THE STAR

THINK LIKE AN NP

Everything you need to know before applying to NP School

DR. PATRICE LITTLE
FOUNDER AND CEO OF NP STUDENT®

The Starter Guide To Think Like An NP: Everything You Need To Know Before Applying To NP School

Copyright © 2024 Patrice Little. All rights reserved.

No part of this book may be reproduced or transmitted in any form or by any means electronic or mechanical photocopying, recording, or by any information storage and retrieval system without the prior written permission of the author, except for the inclusion of brief quotations in critical reviews and certain other noncommercial uses permitted by copyright law.

ISBN: 979-8-9892772-6-1

Photo credit © Jason Grindle Photography

For permission requests, contact the publisher.

Extreme Overflow Publishing

A Brand of Extreme Overflow Enterprises, Inc.

P.O. Box 1811, Dacula, GA 30019

www.extremeoverflow.com

Send feedback to info@extremeoverflow.com

Printed in the United States of America

Library of Congress Catalog in-Publication

Data is available for this title

THE STARTER GUIDE TO
THINK LIKE AN NP

Everything you need to know before applying to NP School

EXTREME OVERFLOW PUBLISHING
DACULA, GA USA

ACKNOWLEDGEMENTS

Writing "The Starter Guide" has been an incredibly liberating experience, and this endeavor would not have been possible without the unwavering support, dedication, and contributions of many remarkable individuals.

To my copyeditor, Miguel Muirhead: Your guidance and steadfast support were invaluable throughout the editing process of this book. Your meticulous attention to detail, along with suggestions for formatting and page layout, has significantly enhanced its readability for students. For this, I am truly grateful.

My publisher, Yolanda Lewis and the entire Extreme Overflow team: Working with such a dynamic and dedicated team has been an enriching experience, and your contributions have been integral to the success of this project.

I am grateful to the contributors: Gale Adcock, Ashley Blackmon, Andrea Brassard, Cherise Carpenter, Celia McIntosh, Cashmere Miller, Adrian Rolle, Brittany Winestock, and Sikangezile Zulu. Thank you for meeting tight deadlines and providing invaluable insights that have enriched the guide immeasurably.

I also want to express my gratitude to Dr. Mavis Schorn at Vanderbilt University for her valuable insights on fostering inclusivity to benefit students and her feedback. Additionally, my thanks go to my fellow from the Academy of Diverse Emerging Nurse Leaders, Christyl Barnes, for reviewing the book and providing feedback from a Generation Z perspective.

Most importantly, special thanks to my children: Kaitlyn and Caleb. Your patience and understanding throughout this process have been the foundation of my strength. You guys are my inspiration, and I am endlessly grateful for the time you sacrificed so I could help others realize their potential and live out their dreams.

To everyone who played a part in bringing "The Starter Guide" to life, thank you from the bottom of my heart.

CONTENTS

Introduction 1

If I Only Knew Then: Insights from Esteemed Nurse Practitioners 4

Chapter 1: What Can You Expect As a Nurse Practitioner 9

Chapter 2: Selecting the Best NP School 30

Chapter 3: Becoming an Ideal Candidate 60

Chapter 4: Time to Apply 76

Chapter 5: The Next Step 82

Glossary 102

End Notes 107

About the Author 114

Introduction

I had three choices. As a first-generation American from a Jamaican family, the expectations were clear: doctor, lawyer, or engineer. These professions were highly esteemed in my culture, embodying financial stability, intellectual accomplishment, and community respect. And so, I originally wanted to be a medical doctor, but I put my own flair on it and became a Doctor of Nursing Practice (DNP).

Just as my path led me to a fulfilling career as a nurse practitioner (NP), your journey toward becoming one will also be filled with unique opportunities and choices. It should not only be informed by others' experiences but also about taking those insights and shaping a path that's best for you. While practical tips for NP school on YouTube, Instagram, and TikTok offer essential guidance for aspiring NPs, they often provide just a piece of the puzzle. The path to becoming involves piecing together many fragments into a complete, informed picture.

An NP is a master's or doctorate-prepared advanced practice registered nurse authorized to diagnose, prescribe, and autonomously treat patients. Becoming an NP was one of the best decisions I made in my life yet the experience was far from smooth. Despite what some of my cohort expressed, that I made NP school look effortless, it was quite the opposite. While I had excellent professors, I still faced challenges in finding my preceptors, and understanding pathophysiology and performing some procedures. Furthermore, despite passing the boards on my first try, my initial experience as an NP in a locum position at an Urgent Care clinic, which mainly involved handling primary care cases, did not go as planned. The reality is that transitioning from registered nurse (RN) to NP can look different for everyone. One thing that remains constant is the need for clear guidance and actionable steps in navigating this complex transition.

Having experienced this transition myself, I understand the nuances and challenges it presents. A key aspect to consider, and one that often marks the biggest difference between an RN and an NP, is the way you think about the level of care you provide to your patients. When you work as an RN, you carry out orders in segmented tasks that are written by a medical doctor (MD), physician associate/assistant (PA), or an NP. Whereas, when you work as an NP, you're thinking from the scope of comprehensive care. This means you are responsible to think through the care that is delivered from the time the patient comes in for a visit until their condition is resolved or maintained. And the rigor of the program you apply to prepares you to think like an NP.

I have come across many social media posts about how being an NP is not what they expected it to be. These posts serve as a reminder that thoughtful consideration and preparation are essential when pursuing any career. Those who are disappointed may not have adequately prepared. Therefore, when you come across similar posts, here's what you should mentally ask:

- Did you do your research?
- Did you ask the right questions before pursuing the NP track?
- Did you feel like your program prepared you for the transition?
- Do you feel like your current position is not the right fit?

This is why I created a three-part series to provide a foundation when it comes to transitioning from RN to NP. You are reading part one. In this guide, we open with 'If I Only Knew Then,' where you'll find invaluable anecdotes generously shared by some of my esteemed NP colleagues from across the nation. I also share insights from my experience as both an instructor and former student to clarify misconceptions and assist you in making a well-informed decision when applying to NP school. Even more, I anonymously highlight students who have benefited from NP Student® products and services. At the end of each chapter, you'll find 'Dr. Little's Prescriptions,' which are actionable steps designed to take you from NP aspiration to acceptance. It is my mission to help you get the information you need to be the NP you have always dreamed about.

If I Only Knew Then: Insights from Esteemed Nurse Practitioners

As I was finalizing this guide, I could not help but reflect on the profound role that my network, mentorship, and the unwavering support of my colleagues played in my career. I owe much of my success to these invaluable connections. For this reason, I invited eight esteemed colleagues to share their stories. What I found was twofold: challenges in navigating the transition from RN to NP have persisted over time, often becoming more pronounced as the NP profession evolved. Additionally, they highlighted aspects of their academic journey that are not commonly addressed on various platforms.

In this section, inspired by the phrase I use to begin my monthly blogs, you'll find a collection of anecdotes. These stories draw from the idea that with life and career progression comes wisdom – insights we often wish we had earlier. Therefore, keep these stories in mind as you progress through the guide to enlighten your own path and empower you on your journey of becoming an NP.

If I only knew then what I know now, I would have sought out mentors both before applying and during my NP program to guide me through the journey. I regret not applying for scholarships while in the program; the demanding workload made it feel like an overwhelming task. I also wish I had taken my science courses more seriously, as they significantly influenced my GPA. Consequently, when I applied to NP school, I was accepted under probationary conditions. Before applying, I wish I had understood the crucial importance of my science grades in the application process.

Celia McIntosh, DNP, RN, FNP-C, PMHNP-BC, SCRN, CCRN, CEN, CNRN

I wish I knew the importance of confirming if an organization for your practicum is affiliated with your school. It's incredibly disheartening to secure a preceptor independently, only to discover later that there's no affiliation with your school, leading to another challenging search. In clinics or private practices where affiliation isn't a concern, the financial cost can be significant. It's often a choice between limited options and high expenses.

Sika Zulu, MSN, FNP-C

Looking back at my NP school application process, I realize I should have conducted more research to identify available scholarships for which I could be eligible as a part-time student. The scholarship from the university I attended was revoked due to my part-time status, as scholarships were only available to full-time students. I would also have considered staying longer with my employer to receive tuition reimbursement.

Cherise Carpenter, MSN, FNP-C

I wish I had known what to expect from each certifying body to better prepare for the boards. It would have been helpful to be aware that each body provides an exam blueprint detailing the current exam's content. This information would have allowed for gradual preparation throughout my schooling. Then, as I prepared for the certification exam, I would be reviewing from a structured base instead of feeling overwhelmed and unsure where to begin.

Brittany Winestock, DNP, FNP-BC

I had an unusual path to becoming an NP – I embarked on this journey after completing my PhD. Initially, I enrolled in the adult NP program at the nursing school where I was a faculty member, as it was the only NP program available there. Years later, after moving to another state, I joined the family NP program at my new faculty school. This required taking additional courses and completing numerous clinical hours in pediatrics, obstetrics, and family medicine. As an FNP, I continued my role as a faculty member while also working weekends in convenient care, which helped fund my stepchildren's higher education.

My advice is to carefully consider your NP specialty choice to avoid the need to complete extra courses and clinical hours.

Andrea Brassard, PhD, FNP-BC, FAANP, FAAN, CNE

Due to the restrictive practice laws in my state, I wish I had realized how challenging it would be to find a job in primary care. I had focused my studies on family practice, thinking it would enhance my marketability. Unfortunately, this choice actually made finding the right practice more difficult. It's important to research your state's practice laws thoroughly and talk to different NPs in various roles about their experiences. Be aware that your 'dream job' may not be readily available, or your preferences may change, and you'll need to adapt to those changes.

Ashley Blackmon, MSN, FNP-C

Reflecting on my path to becoming a nurse practitioner, I now realize the significance of understanding the legal aspects associated with the role. Specifically, topics such as Drug Enforcement Administration (DEA) registration, billing and coding, and familiarity with CMS proved to be pivotal elements in my NP journey. While my educational program laid a solid foundation in clinical skills, it didn't emphasize these essential components of NP practice enough. Gaining early insights into these legal considerations could have better prepared me for the comprehensive responsibilities of being an NP.

Adrian Rolle, DNP, APRN, FNP-C

Thinking back to when I was preparing for my NP program, I wish I would have become involved with my local nurse practitioner organization early on to leverage support for desirable clinical placements, job seeking, and to build my professional network.

Cashmere Miller, DNP, APRN, FNP-C

How much nursing experience to have before NP school was not a significant concern when I entered my graduate program in 1985. During my nursing school days, I didn't hear much about NPs and, once practicing, observed few NPs in action. This lack of exposure is why most of my MSN cohort had over a decade of experience in hospitals and outpatient settings like public health before entering graduate school. I noted then, as I believe now, that our expertise as RNs facilitated our transition to novice NPs. Our mastery of nursing fundamentals —hands-on care, critical thinking, autonomous decision-making, interprofessional collaboration, and patient advocacy —provided a solid foundation for acquiring new knowledge and skills in graduate school. Even with occasional uncertainties in learning to diagnose, treat, and perform procedures, we were confident, knowing we weren't starting from scratch. This confidence stemmed from the depth and quality of our experience, not merely its duration.

My advice for those aspiring to become NPs is this: base your readiness on more than a measurement of time. Being prepared to dive into the rigors of an NP program and function as a confident novice NP depends more on what you've been doing as a nurse than how long you've been doing it. If your nursing practice has not built a strong skill set as well as confidence in what you know and don't know—if you are still functioning as a Registered Nurse novice—you don't have the foundation needed to learn to practice as an Advanced Practice Registered Nurse (APRN). This disadvantage won't just affect how much you struggle in your program—it will affect patients entrusted to your care as a student and new NP and impact the provider team you will eventually work alongside. This may be hard to hear if you feel pressured to "get going" in your career or suffer from a fear of missing out (FOMO), but all signs point to plenty of NP program availability and job opportunities for NPs. Take a step back, do a self-analysis, and fill those gaps with experiences in settings that prepare you to be a strong NP student, a confident novice NP, and eventually an expert NP.

Gale Adcock MSN, FNP-BC, FAANP, FAAN

Chapter 1
What can you expect as a nurse practitioner?

Begin with the end in mind.
Franklin Covey

Key Points

- Starting with the end in mind makes the application process smoother.
- Prior RN clinical experience leads to comfort, and comfort leads to NP experience.
- The diversity of your experiences and backgrounds is a strength, not just a prerequisite.
- Before applying, consider the key elements of NP student life: finances, networking, and personal development.

I have been a nurse practitioner (NP) for over a decade and have enjoyed every moment of it, even the parts that weren't cute. I remember when I was getting ready to apply to NP school. I felt I reached the height of my registered nurse (RN) career and becoming an NP was the next best step. It was also my destination. However, I had my concerns about whether I would be accepted into a program. Mainly, I only had eight months of RN clinical experience, and, at the time, many schools required at least two years of clinical experience for admission.

Like most RN graduates, I started my career on the Medical Surgical (Med-Surg) floor. I was encouraged to start here to develop my fundamental nursing skills. However, I would have never expected that I would feel unfilled and burnt-out working Med-Surg in a short time.

Fortunately, I was able to use my transferable skills gained from teaching high school to segue into nursing administrative roles such as birth to five coordinator and case manager to name a few. I did not expect to find a variety of RN positions that focused on non-clinical responsibilities such as care coordination with case management (a more familiar term), state immunization program's coordinator, and birth to 5 coordinator. In total, I worked as an RN for three years before applying to NP school.

RN Experience Before NP School

Many RNs have asked, in various ways, "Do I have to work as an RN before going to NP school?" I often share a story as part of my response because I've found a blatant response with no examples or evidential support is the least received. More so, my goal is to encourage nurses to see themselves in the story or circumstance to help make an informed decision.

I once precepted a new NP in the urgent care at a county jail. I was shocked she could barely get through her patient's assessment without asking me if she was doing it correctly.

This was terrifying because urgent care providers had the greatest responsibility at this jail. We were responsible for establishing the baseline of new patients (inmates) with medical conditions and management of acute and chronic conditions, as well as injuries. We were also responsible for overseeing the care for about 2500 patients. Of course, we were supported with the help of our care team and security. Above all, everyone looked to us as the decision makers and my preceptee was not prepared for this duty.

It wasn't until our debriefing, that I found out she attended a proprietary NP school with no RN experience, received most of her training online, and was responsible for finding her own clinical placement. She expressed she didn't feel her program prepared her for practice. This is when I realized how having little to no RN experience is more about a risk to patients and not merely a way to create a barrier to those who want to start their NP journey right away. Even more, her school was known to not produce competent practitioners.

Here are the facts, a head-to-toe assessment is the bread and butter of primary care all patients receive. As an NP, you can expect to perform an initial, focused, emergency, or a follow-up health assessment as part of your care. Some settings, such as retail clinics, require NPs to check in patients, take vitals, perform an assessment, do point of care testing, administer medications when indicated, and provide patient education. Therefore, you are expected to be knowledgeable, have strong critical thinking, time-management, and decision-making skills.

In NP school, nurses build upon their RN foundation or competencies to one day give orders and perform comprehensive care. How can one build upon a skill they have not developed? Does it benefit the patient when the provider is not competent? Is there a high probability that you could jeopardize your career?

These are just a few questions I ask at the end of sharing this story. Naturally, there are exceptions to the rule, and they exist because of factors such as the nurse is a fast learner, worked in a clinical setting in a different health profession, received training from a state-of-the-art school, and more. Undoubtedly, the implicit rule to have RN experience first is not supported by any evidence but educators' perception that prior RN clinical experience is predictive of academic success as an NP student.[1,2,3] It is based on what to expect as a nurse practitioner.

Case in point, when it comes to the RN clinical experience before NP school debate, I favor the side that is best for the patient. If you are not comfortable performing essential parts of care, then seek out more experience until you can do it without putting the patient or your license at risk.

Pathways to NP

Today, we, NP faculty, have a better understanding of the NP pathways. Nurses who advance towards becoming NPs bring with them a variety of backgrounds and experiences, enriching the diversity of our workforce. Hence, my goal is to guide you in finding your unique pathway to becoming an NP.

My journey to becoming an NP started in 2001. I started exploring the NP role, as a volunteer, when I was one year away from completing my Biology Pre-medicine degree. I learned what the day in the life of an NP as a volunteer at Georgia Southwestern State University's student health center. I observed skills and responsibilities such as physical assessments, maintaining confidentiality, restocking of clinical supplies, and maintaining cleanliness of the exam rooms. This was very similar to the role I had as an NP at Consumer Value Store (CVS) Minute Clinic 20 years later. I expected to diagnose common health conditions and diseases, prescribe certain medications and treatment plans, educate and counsel patients and their families, and evaluate responses to treatment.

Looking back, I was privileged to have the opportunity to see it and feel it before becoming it. I knew what to expect as an NP. This is my hope for you and why I recommend shadowing an NP to explore the different facets of the role before applying. Now is the time.

For High School Students

As a high school student aspiring to become an NP, start by focusing on a foundation in science. Taking Advanced Placement (AP) classes in biology, chemistry, and psychology can provide a head start, as these subjects are integral to nursing education. Additionally, participating in extracurricular activities like health science clubs or volunteering at local healthcare facilities can offer practical insights into the healthcare field. Mathematics, particularly statistics, is also beneficial, as it forms a significant part of evidence-based practice (the process of making decisions combining the best research, clinical experience, and what patients want to make the best care decisions) in nursing.

From here, I encourage you to participate in a pre-nursing summer camp for high school students to further explore nursing. More and more hospitals and nursing schools have launched these programs to not only introduce you to nursing concepts but also provide hands-on nursing basics. Our *Think Like an NP Bootcamp for Teens* offers introductory, hands-on nursing experiences and a customized roadmap for aspiring students. Visit our website for more on upcoming sessions!

Finally, nursing programs often look for well-rounded individuals with a demonstrated interest in healthcare and community welfare. My advice is to engage in community service and leadership roles, as these can further strengthen your college applications, whether you pursue nursing or not.

For Career Changers/Non-Nurses

Changing careers one to three times in life is common. For those looking to transition to nursing from another field, understanding the prerequisites for nursing programs is essential. If you have a bachelor's degree in a non-nursing field, consider accelerated or direct-entry Master of Science in Nursing (MSN) programs for non-nurses (**Table 1**). These programs often require courses in human anatomy, physiology, microbiology, and sometimes nutrition or statistics. Plan to include these courses in your transition.

Before starting the ABSN program at Georgia Southwestern State University, I took statistics and microbiology online at Darton College (now known as Darton College of Health Professionals at Albany State University). In 2005, I was also fortunate to participate in the Health Careers Opportunity Program (HCOP) at Albany State University. HCOP, a grant-funded federal program under the Health Resources and Services Administration (HRSA), provides funds to colleges to assist aspiring health professionals from disadvantaged backgrounds to enter and graduate from health and allied health professions schools.

It is also important to mention that the need for nurse practitioners is so great that individuals with a non-nursing background can pursue a path to becoming an NP through PreSpecialty master's entry programs.[4]

Table 1. Pathways to Nurse Practitioner and years to complete.

Pathway	Description	Typical Candidates	Estimated Years (Depending on enrollment status)
Traditional BSN to MSN	BSN degree, RN licensure, clinical experience, then MSN focusing on NP specialty/major.	High school graduates or early-career nurses such as certified nurses assistants (CNAs) and licensed practical/vocational nurses (LPN/LVNs)	6-9 years (4 years for BSN, 1-2 years experience, 1-3 years for MSN)
ADN to BSN to NP Bridge	ADN degree, RN work, BSN (RN-to-BSN program), then MSN focusing on a specialization.	Nurses with an ADN seeking to advance to an NP	8-11 years (2-3 years for ADN, 1-2 years work, 1-2 years for BSN, 1-3 years for MSN)
Direct Entry for Non-Nurses	Non-nursing bachelor's degree to foundational nursing education, then a MSN with specialization.	Career changers with a non-nursing bachelor's degree.	3-6 years (1-2 years pre-licensure, 2-4 years for MSN)
Dual Role/ Dual Focus Programs	Combined clinical specialties or dual roles, MSN or DNP, focusing on multiple specializations.	Nurses seeking broad or multiple specializations.	6-9 years (varies based on education background and the program structure)

Post-Master's Certificate	Additional NP specialization for MSN-prepared NP	Experienced NPs or MSN nurses seeking an additional speciality or a nurse practitioner certificate.	1-3 years (depending on specialty and program type)
Post-Master's DNP	MSN degree required or BSN as part of a BSN-to-DNP program track	RNs or NPs aiming for the highest level of clinical practice, leadership, or wanting to implement evidence-based practice at a systemic level.	3-6 years post-BSN (1-3 years for MSN if not already obtained, plus 2-3 years for DNP)

Is it a good time to become an NP?

I am confident that this is a prime time to pursue becoming an NP, as a registered nurse (RN). For starters, many sources show that the NP profession is one career that will survive the next 10 years. Also, the NP profession has ranked in the top five of Best Health Care Jobs in the U.S. News and World Report for the past five years.[5] In addition, the NP workforce grew by 8.5% in 2023 and is expected to grow by 45% by 2032.[6] The claim of job security and growth as a NP is well supported.

However, in the past six years, new NP graduates in Atlanta have shared that FNP positions are oversaturated. Meaning the available primary care positions are little to not available in the city. If this is applicable to your region, understand that the Family NP specialty is oversaturated and is more so dependent on factors such as the city, state, or region where you practice. It is not a reflection of the national need for providers. In fact, there are ample opportunities to work in underserved and rural communities. This point further solidifies that over-saturation in the NP profession is regional. For this reason, I recommend exploring the trends of where you desire to practice before you even decide to explore schools.

When you become an NP, you are equipped to provide quality care from the top and make a difference. At the same time, you have a higher risk of malpractice in a position with more autonomy. Whether you decide to apply today or tomorrow, the potential to secure flexible, versatile, highly compensated opportunities for the next 10 years is promising.

Getting Start

Beginning to apply starts with the end in mind, and I want you to think about what you want your end to look like. This approach is indispensable for making the application process smoother. For me, I wanted my NP school to be close to home, flexible schedule, small cohort, and a supportive faculty. This was my search criteria for schools. Once I identified a couple of schools that I was interested in, I attended their interest meetings to get a deeper understanding of their program's structure and how it would fit in my life as a wife, mother, and full-time RN. Then I applied to one school and was accepted on the first attempt. Reflecting on what I know now, the path I chose was perfect for my personal and professional development. It allowed me the necessary time to learn and prepare for NP practice.

There are two things I would have added to my application journey to better prepare for NP school. First, I would have found my preceptors early or attended a school that offered preceptor placement. A preceptor is an experienced practitioner who provides supervision during clinical training and facilitates the application of theory to practice. There is a consensus among the NP community that there is a lack of accessible preceptors. Even more, there is a lack of standardized clinical training, and we will discuss more in book two. The last thing I would have added to my journey would have been requesting a tuition discount to pay out of pocket or applying for scholarships throughout the program. Many students are unaware that their tuition can be negotiated. I did not learn about this until I did a feature on *Graduating NP School Debt Free* for NP Student® magazine. In fact, it was the top frequently viewed article. And what I know for sure is that if you do not take time to prepare to pay for tuition on the front end, you will face it again on the back end. For this reason, I recommend having an in-depth understanding of these three aspects before applying to NP school: financial, networking, and personal development.

Financial

Attending NP school is a financial investment for your future. According to the United States (U.S.) Bureau of Labor Statistics (BLS), the median annual wage of NPs in 2022 was $121,610 as compared to the median annual wage of an RN which is $81,220.[7] The annual wage is calculated based on year-round full-time status. Therefore, overtime is not factored in the equation, and the difference in salary between the two professions is $40,000. Therefore, becoming an NP has a positive return on investment (ROI).

There are many options to cover your tuition for NP school and the method you choose is up to you.[8] I've interacted with thousands of students on my platform who've expressed they were unaware of all their options. In fact, most students shared that they covered their tuition with a combination of financial resources such as grants, scholarships, federal student loans, private student loans, tuition reimbursement through their employer, and out of pocket. Other financial resources include fellowships, work study, student loan repayment, education debt reduction program, loan forgiveness, teaching assistant opportunities, and a tuition free NP program. Yes, you've read correctly. To date, the University of Pennsylvania (UPenn) offers a tuition free NP program for nurses.[9] In exchange for funding, UPenn's nurses agree to work two years in an underserved area. If you are one who is willing to commit to this agreement, then this would be a program for you. However, be mindful that most commitments that require service at a critical shortage facility in exchange for tuition assistance will require reimbursement if you choose not to keep your commitment. I believe that this approach is fair because they are investing in you as a student.

Federal Financial Aid

It is also important to mention that there is federal funding to prepare the next wave of NPs to replace those who are leaving the workforce due to retirement or other pursuits. Navigating the labyrinth of financial aid options does not have to be a daunting task. Here are the essentials you should know:

FAFSA: Start with the Free Application for Federal Student Aid (FAFSA). Completing the FAFSA form is essential to apply for federal student aid like grants, work-study, and loans, and it's a key step in securing funds for college in general. Your FAFSA information is also used by states, colleges, and some private aid providers to determine your eligibility for various types of funding.[10]

Grants vs. Loans: Grants are free money you don't have to repay, while loans must be paid back with interest. Both can come from the federal government, state agencies, or private institutions.

Service-Cancelable Loans: These are special types of loans that can be canceled if you work in high-need areas after graduation. Usually, these are rural or underserved communities.

Institutional Scholarships

Many NP schools offer scholarships based on academic merit or financial need. Consult your school's financial aid office for more information.

Private Scholarships

Organizations often offer scholarships to healthcare students. Research and apply widely—every dollar counts.

Tuition Reimbursement

Some healthcare employers will cover a portion of your tuition in return for a commitment to work for them after graduation. For many nurses on the brink of becoming NPs, tuition reimbursement is a compelling option. This employer-sponsored program essentially allows you to "earn while you learn," transforming your current workplace into a stepping stone for your advanced practice role.

How It Works

- Contractual Agreement: Typically, you'll enter into a contractual agreement with your employer, committing to work for a specified period in exchange for partial or complete tuition coverage.
- Reimbursement vs. Upfront Payment: Some programs reimburse you after successful course completion, while others might pay tuition costs upfront.

Eligibility

- Tenure: Many programs require you to be employed for a certain period before becoming eligible.

- Academic Performance: Maintaining a minimum GPA might be a requirement for continued sponsorship.

Benefits
- Financial Relief: The obvious advantage is the minimization or elimination of out-of-pocket expenses.
- Career Advancement: Organizations that offer tuition reimbursement often provide growth opportunities, effectively creating a pipeline from RN to NP within the same institution.

Limitations
- Commitment: You're usually required to remain with the employer for a predetermined period post-graduation.
- Limited Scope: Some employers will only fund programs that are directly aligned with their business needs, which might limit your specialization choices.

Best Practices
- Read the Fine Print: Understand the terms and conditions before agreeing to any sponsorship deal.
- Consult HR: Your Human Resources department is a valuable resource for navigating the complexities of tuition reimbursement programs.

Military Options

For those willing to commit to military service, scholarships and service-cancelable loans are available, along with substantial signing bonuses. Requirements vary by branch. The Department of Defense or the military is another option you can use to pay for NP school. When you sign up for one of the four branches: Army, Marines, Navy, and Air Force (**Table 2**) you are committing to serving. Therefore, the requirements are straightforward like it is for most civilian positions except there is an age requirement. The age requirement is between 18 and 47[11,12] Be sure to check the website periodically to verify the current education, clinical experience, and age requirement.

There are advantages and disadvantages to this route. The notable advantages that attract most nurses are job security, great compensation, and growth opportunities. When you enter the service with a degree you enter as an officer. Therefore, you can expect to take an Officer Training course to be completed as part of the requirements. In many instances, nurses receive sign-on bonuses. The disadvantage to serving is time spent away from family, having to stay until service time is complete, and no control over your assignment.

There are also subprograms such as the Nurse Corps through the U.S. Army that provide financial assistance for NP schools. The U.S. Army Medical Department ranks as one of the most extensive comprehensive health care systems in the United States.[11,12] There are also opportunities to work for the U.S. Department of Veteran Affairs also offers tuition assistance programs and student loan repayment program (SLRP). If this interests you, you can connect with a recruiter via the branch's website.

Always consult the respective military branch websites or a recruiter for the most current information.

Is the military service pathway a feasible route for you? Could it serve as the cornerstone in your journey to becoming an NP, while simultaneously expanding your horizons on a global scale?

Table 2. Requirements for entering the U.S. military as a nurse.[12,13,14,15]

Branch	Description	Requirement
Army	Offers Nurse Corps with specialized financial aid for NP school. Known for its comprehensive healthcare system.	Age 18-47, Bachelor of Science in Nursing (BSN), pass the NCLEX-RN, and meet the specific clinical experience criteria.
Marine	The Marines rely on the Navy for medical support but offer healthcare career opportunities through the Naval Reserve.	Age 18-47, Must qualify for the Navy's Medical programs (BSN and NCLEX-RN required), and meet specific clinical experience criteria.
Navy	Known for its Nurse Candidate Program and offering scholarships for future service.	Age 18-41, BSN and NCLEX-RN, specific clinical experience criteria, and successful completion of a Navy Officer Program.
Airforce	Provides extensive opportunities for specialization and research in healthcare	Age 18-47, BSN and NCLEX-RN, meet specific clinical experience criteria, and complete the Air Force Officer Training School.

Tuition Payment Options

If you plan to pay out of pocket, plan for expected and unexpected costs. In general, books and tuition are expected. However, when it comes to healthcare degrees, other expenses such as your commute to the clinical training site, Basic Life Support (BLS) certification, lab coat, clinical tracking systems (Typhon), snacks, and in some cases, preceptorships can add up quickly. Many schools offer alternative payment plans where you can prepay, or Another option is paying your tuition in installments over time. Some students opt to pay monthly or quarterly for the academic year. if you can't front the cost at the beginning of the semester. Lastly, I encourage you to contact the financial aid office for specifics on tuition payment options.

Lastly, consult with a financial advisor to create a budget so paying out of pocket can work for you and your family. Overall, it's about putting everything in perspective before you're required to act.

So, what's your game plan? How will you fund your dream of becoming an NP? Remember, the end goal is not just about financing an education but also about sustaining a lifestyle conducive to academic success.

Networking

Prior to starting NP Student® there were no platforms solely dedicated to NP students that could advocate on their behalf and help them navigate the day-to-day issues of NP school. Although joining a professional organization or association has its benefits, it is important to join one that aligns with your career goals. I did not have time to be actively involved in an NP organization while in school. In fact, most of my students mentioned that they typically have free time before NP school and the breaks between the semesters. I would be remiss if I didn't suggest joining your local or national NP association before starting NP school to establish rapport. Take advantage of the benefits you can receive with a student or career starter membership. Your involvement would entail attending chapter monthly meetings, annual conferences, or symposiums. In addition, you are in proximity to practicing NPs who may be willing to serve as a mentor.

Networking not only sets you up for a potential preceptor or job opportunities, but it also prepares you for using your network as a clinical resource for practice. For instance, I had a patient who had recurrent bacterial vaginosis and I consulted with my colleague who works in Women's Health for an alternative treatment that was successful. Of course, I verified the treatment option but if it wasn't for my colleague,

I would have referred my patient out which would have cost her more time and money. In the end, my goal was to provide quality care for the best outcome. Similarly, medical doctors consult with each other when they encounter something outside of their specialty. This is what makes having a network a win for patients too.

Today, many students use social media for networking. When I was in NP school, I never considered using social media for networking because I didn't have time for it and did not know how to leverage it. Also, Facebook groups didn't start until a couple months after I began NP school. Instagram was just pictures only. TikTok did not exist. I viewed LinkedIn as a platform for established professionals only. All the platforms have evolved to be educational as well as entertaining. I will discuss more on how engaging on social media can be detrimental to your future career as an NP.

Developing relationships with current NP students in the cohort ahead of you has its advantages as well. For me, I received inspiration and preceptor connection from friends I gained in the previous cohort. This form of networking is also known as college networking which prepares you to develop communication skills needed for interacting with professionals in the future. In fact, after I graduated NP school, I pitched a preceptor exchange program to the Dean of Brenau University. Unfortunately, nothing came out of it. I originally got the idea from my younger sister who is a physician. She was in medical school while I was in NP school, and we would compare our experiences. The one thing that her medical school embraced was networking. I recommend networking early and networking often. If you don't gain a preceptor at least you gained a relationship. For this reason, nurturing your relationships is just as important as establishing them.

Personal Development

Pursuing advanced education such as NP is a form of personal development. The educational process is transformational. Keep in mind that it is also continuous, requires patience, and involves discovery. Most college career centers provide a career assessment (Type Focus, Strong Interest Inventory, O*Net Interest Profiler) as a part of their career planning service. I took an assessment as an undergraduate. It was on point.

I believe a college's career center is the most underutilized resource that helps students learn more about their personalities, interests, and create a development plan. From here, by volunteering and shadowing. Again, this is the closest you will get to observing the role you desire and interviewing a practicing NP to get some credible answers. Remember, it is not enough to visualize yourself in the NP role but try to feel it to become it.

Another resource is taking the NP LifeFit Test to see if NP school is for you. In fact, I created this tool in 2019 as the point of entry to my summer program and consultations. It mentally positions students before NP school. The goal is for students to identify their blind spots in life and connect to resources so they can get the most out of their learning experience. This prevents them from feeling behind before they get started. I can assure you that if you do not like the responsibilities that come with being an NP and if you are unclear of who you are and what you want, chances are NP school may be a challenge. You'll learn more about this tool in Chapter 5.

If you are not currently enrolled in school, I also encourage you to take the Myers-Briggs Type Indicator (MBTI) test to learn more about your personality. According to this test, there are 16 personality types based on a list of preferences.[16,17] It helps you understand how you view the world, interact with people, and identify your strengths and weaknesses. This test also provides career options that fit well with the identified personalities. Being aware of how personalities like yours approach life can be helpful when it comes to working as an NP who oversees patients' health and their staff.

I took this test when I was at a crossroads in my life. At the time, I was an NP for two years, and I felt like my life was mundane. It was weird because I enjoyed where I worked and my patients but still felt unfulfilled. It wasn't until I discovered my personality type is an ENFJ-A that I gained a sense of clarity and hired a coach to help me navigate my next steps in life.

Here is how ENFJ-A is interpreted.

   a. **Strength of individual traits:** Extraverted: 80%, Intuitive: 56%, Feeling: 74%, Judging: 61%, Assertive: 75%.
   b. **Role:** Diplomat
   c. **Strategy:** People Mastery.

From here, I realized that I needed to be challenged in my current role. A couple of years later, I started NP Student®. In fact, I created this opportunity. In this role, I get to interact with many students, help them navigate their life and career, and advocate on their behalf. In addition, I provide guidance for NPs, like me, who become stuck in their journey. Trust me, take the test.

For now, we can plan for your application by first looking at the dream NP job you want to identify key skills, qualifications, and experiences that qualify you for the role. After all, applying for your dream job is the end point of your journey. For this reason, doing your research on the front end saves time and helps you make an informed decision. I also understand as you matriculate in the program your dream job may change and that's ok. The goal is to be ready to apply for a job once you are finished with the program and have passed boards. Every discipline has a culture. The culture of the NP workforce has many unspoken rules and knowing what to expect before you get there early in your journey is a plus.

Dr. Little's Prescription:

Find your dream NP job online. What do you notice about the job description?* What stands out in the requirements?

*Please note some job descriptions may start off listing the expectations as "You will" somewhat like an objective.

Chapter 2
Selecting the Best NP School

The best NP school is the one that aligns with your core values and goals.

Key Points

- 💡 If you want the best NP school, you will need to vet their accreditation status, preceptor placement process, graduation rates, board exam passing rates, and alignment with core values, among other key factors.
- 💡 To save time and money, familiarize yourself with NP specialties: pros, cons, job outlook, compensation.
- 💡 Pursuing a DNP—right away or with experience—has pros and cons.
- 💡 If you seek diverse NP career paths, consider non-traditional roles such as telehealth and aesthetics.

Emily, fresh out of her BSN program, reached out to me with a question I often hear from aspiring NPs. She knew she wanted to become a Family Nurse Practitioner (FNP) but was overwhelmed by the plethora of schools and specializations available. In addition, her questions about program quality, tuition costs, and balancing her personal and professional life were daunting. As someone who has walked this path and mentored others through it, I could relate to her dilemma; it's a crossroads many in our field encounter. In a discovery session, we examined her options, grounding them in her personal and professional aspirations. From here, it became clear that choosing the right NP program was a significant decision for Emily, as it is for you.

So, where does one begin in this when selecting the best NP school? A good first step is to consult the U.S. News and World Report, which offers an essential guide for comparing top-notch schools based on 15 ranking factors.[1] The ranking factors include faculty resources, quality assessment, program size, student selectivity. It serves as a tool for you to compare schools and filter your search based on program type, tuition, enrollment. You can create an account for a fee to gain access to the acceptance rate, degrees offered, and to save your favorite schools. This information is obtained via a survey. However, keep in mind that out of 648 schools with masters and doctorate programs, only 246 schools who were invited participated in the survey.[1] Nonetheless, you are preparing to think comprehensively as an NP and should consider looking into as other factors as possible to fully vet or research a prospective school.

I've found that the vetting process is individualized, and the best NP school is the one that aligns with your core values and goals. I cannot emphasize enough that two applicants are not on the same journey. For some, selecting the best school may not be based on quality of the education and the ease of the admission process. However, if the school is associated with quality education and training, it may have a more enriched application process. If it starts not to look like you'll have a quality experience, consider looking into another school. You can start with the in-person information session or virtual event. This is where you can learn more about the programs offered, admission process, and additional information that may not be listed on their website.

I attended a couple of information sessions before I selected a school. In my search I was looking for a program that offered a small class size, near my home, and with a flexible schedule. Your top school may not be someone else's top school. It is based on what you prioritize as important.

How do you choose? I encourage you to use the same approach you did when researching your undergraduate school. That's if you researched your undergraduate program. Mainly, my students expressed that they were disappointed in a few areas but because they started the program, they continued until the end. That's why, I decided to list out what you should make priority in your research to avoid disappointment. Then decide on the nonnegotiable to help you narrow in your selection of the top two to three schools.

Here are the following areas to research when vetting an NP School:

Accreditation

Always start with verifying the schools' accreditation status and the agency who accredits them. Accreditation proves that an NP program has been approved and held to the highest standards of advanced nursing education. A nursing program's accreditation requires an evaluation of several factors, including the curriculum, the faculty's credentials, and students' retention rates to name a few. Knowing a school's accreditation states can save you money and time. It makes students eligible to apply for financial aid. Accreditation also ensures patient safety. Mainly, all NP graduates are required to take a national certification and nursing license. You can find the accrediting agency logo displayed on most schools' websites on their school or college of nursing landing page. However, if you are unable to find the school's accreditation information on their website, you can search accredited nursing programs under each agency.

Currently, there are two NP accrediting organizations: the Accreditation Commission for Education in Nursing (ACEN) and the Commission on Collegiate Nursing Education (CCNE).[2,3] Please note these organizations also accredits other educational levels of nursing. CCNE accredits from baccalaureates to Doctor of Nursing practice (DNP). Whereas ACEN accredits from practical nursing to DNP. The National League of Nursing (NLN) Commission for Nursing Education Accreditation (CNEA) also accredits DNP programs.[4] However, the primary focus is on nursing and nurse practitioner education.

You've probably heard the horror stories of students who spent years training to become a nurse only to find out that their school's accreditation was withdrawn just before graduation. This is what happened to 200 Lehman College NP students in 2020. Lehman College's NP program lost their accreditation because the average NP board exam passing rate for the past three years fell below 80%.[5,6] In brief, the passing rate is calculated by the number of NP graduates who took the exam divided by the number of NP graduates who passed the exam. That year 45 students completed their NP coursework and were eligible for graduation. The argument was that the program was accredited by the state. This means students could obtain licensure to practice locally. However, national certification makes NPs eligible to practice across the nation if they have a license in that state. The students petitioned for a good cause extension since they were unaware of the school's probation. As a result, the accreditation withdrawal date was extended to March 2021 making the 45 students eligible to sit for boards.[6] For this reason, accreditation matters not only ensures safe practitioners, it also supports a school's mission.

Mission Statement

A mission statement is a distinct public statement that describes an institution's goals and values.[7] It keeps faculty and staff accountable while informing how funds benefit students and shape the program's direction. Interestingly, some nursing programs have a separate mission statement from their parent institution. For most schools, these mission statements embody health education, research, and

---

GBCN Mission Statement

The mission of Georgia Baptist College of Nursing (GBCN) is to excel in teaching, scholarship, leadership, practice, research, and service, while embracing the core values of the College.

Core Values

Excellence — Diligent pursuit of distinction
Christian caring — To value and support all persons.
Compassion — Response to suffering that motivates one to help.
Civility — Respectful behavior toward others
Integrity — Steadfast adherence to honesty and fairness
Collaboration — Working cooperatively to achieve shared goals.
Social responsibility — Commitment to act for the benefit of society.

care delivery.[7,8] It influences the direction of the program and the type of care they want their nurses to provide the community.

I encourage you to write a personal mission statement that describes your purpose and goals. Even more, get clear on your core values or what guides you personally and professionally. Knowing your value makes it easier to decide on the best school for you.

The mission and core values of Georgia Baptist College of Nursing at Mercer University in Atlanta, GA aligned with mine.[8] If anything, their program clarified my purpose in NP policy, practice, and education. That's what I hope the school you choose does for you. Let's look at their mission statement and core values.

All students are expected to embody GBCN's core values. This is demonstrated across their involvement in local and global health activities. I also suggest looking into the school's research interest especially if you plan on pursuing a doctorate.

To select the best candidate, admissions officers and faculty are looking for applicants who closely embody the school's values. This information is often expressed in one's personal statement. On the contrary, a school's mission statement may not hold value to students who just want to be in and out. I would suggest not being this student.

Admission test scores

Since the Coronavirus Disease 2019 (COVID-19) pandemic, a growing number of graduate schools have waived the requirement of the Graduate Record Examination (GRE).[9] It is important to see if your school requires this standardized test as part of their admission process before you apply.

There are two types of GRE test: General and Subject. The GRE General test is the most common which measures verbal reasoning, quantitative reasoning, and analytical writing. It is not an entrance exam per se but is required for admission to graduate school and NP school is a graduate program. Therefore, we will focus on preparation for the GRE general.

Like most standardized tests, the more you practice the more comfortable you'll become with taking the test. You will also gain a better understanding of how you should pace yourself when you take the real test.

Here are a few questions should find an answer for in your research:

1. **Minimum passing score.** What test score are they looking for?
2. **Expiration date.** How old can the scores be if you've already taken the test?
3. **Due date**. When are your scores due?
4. **School Code**: What is the school code for the school you want to receive the results from?

I used to practice the GRE at the Kaplan Testing site in Atlanta. It is a great resource. To date, it cost $220 to take the GRE. I recommend visiting www.gre.com each year to stay abreast on the cost to test, testing centers, and test format. Keep in mind that if the school no longer requires a GRE score, they may request an interview or additional writing as part of their admissions process.

National NP Certification Exam Passing Rates

Taking a national board examination for your certification is the next step after graduation. The two national examinations are American Nurses Credentialing Center

(ANCC) a subsidiary of the American Nurses Association (ANA) and American Academy of Nurse Practitioners (AANP). In brief, the minimum passing score for the AANP exam on a scale of 200 to 800 is 500.[10] The scores vary for the different NP specialties for ANCC. The minimum passing score for the ANCC exam is 85%.[11] The school's exam pass rate should be above 80%. Once the school falls below, they are at risk of losing their accreditation. Sometimes the NP Board Exam passing rates can be found listed on the nursing school's website, under frequently asked questions, or as a downloadable fact sheet. We will build on the details of these two exams in book three.

Program Length

There are many factors that determine the length or duration of your program. Varying sources state the length of NP school can vary from one to six years. Factors that influence duration include but are not limited to full-time and part-time status, the degree you are entering the program with, the specialty you choose, availability of preceptorships, and competing life commitments.

The length of Emory's Family Nurse Practitioner program for a full-time BSN candidate is a whopping one year! Now that the DNP degree is nearing the entry level to NP education, you can expect to commit to a minimum of three years if you have a BSN degree and attend full-time. Whereas you may be in school for a minimum of four years if you enter with an Associate (ASN) of Science in Nursing degree.

I attended my program for three years as part-time status. The program felt like it was never going to end. Yet, I have no regrets. It was perfect for my lifestyle. The biggest challenge I experienced was when a faculty member speculated that my preceptor was not licensed and threatened that I would have to stop my women's health clinicals and redo the next semester. This was a threat to my time and livelihood. I advocated for myself. The faculty did additional research and to this day, I have no idea how things were resolved. All I know is that your school can slack on vetting your preceptor and come back to stop your clinicals. The stress from the threat alone was gruesome. Now imagine if there was truth to their claim. I would have had to watch my colleagues progress through the program while I catch up on clinical hours. To sum up, inquire about preceptor placement to avoid prolonging your program duration by waiting a semester or a year to complete your clinicals.

Preceptor Placement

Preceptorships, also called clinical practicums, clinicials, or hands-on training, is the period where you apply advanced nursing theory into practice. Regardless of which school you choose, you are required to complete a preceptorship. The challenge is most NP schools do not provide a preceptor. Therefore, students dread the stressors of having to find a preceptor, especially when they do not work in a clinical space. That was my issue in NP school. As mentioned, I was far removed from the direct care or the clinical space, I had no interactions with MDs, PAs, or NPs. During the information session, my NP school assured me that they would assist with preceptor placement, and I didn't vet this feature to understand what they truly meant by "providing assistance." Only to find out later in the program that they had a list of past preceptors and students were expected to start with the list first, then find a preceptor on their own if one was not available. Well, to my knowledge, I had classmates who inquired about the list early and were able to lock in their preceptors. I must say, they must have been thoroughly informed because they came ready. This is why I wrote this book.

Finding preceptors is time consuming and schools created a preceptor coordinator role or similar because it requires continuous dedication. Do not get trapped into the "we provide assistance" scheme. Treat the vetting of preceptor placement like a job interview. Ask the schools to walk you through scenarios. Here are a few questions that come to mind:

1. Can you provide more information on how your program assists students with finding a preceptor?
2. Is there a faculty member solely dedicated to finding preceptors for every student?
3. If a student starts off with a preceptor who changes jobs, how do you address it so that the student can smoothly transition with another preceptor and complete clinicals on schedule?
4. Do you have a preceptor exchange program?

The most disappointing thing when it came to finding preceptors was not the disrespect from the physicians during cold calls, it was the immense pressure trying to find a preceptor because completing the program depends on it. Lastly, paying to have access to a preceptor directory only to find out the list was outdated. Many of the preceptors I contacted were either no longer at the site or the contact information changed. This was an unnecessary expense. If you plan to attend a school that does not assist with preceptorship or clinical training placement, the best way to prepare is to start networking now and network often.

Learning Environment

The three types of learning environments or class type are traditional, hybrid, and online. I opted for a hybrid or blended learning environment which entails both synchronous and asynchronous learning options. Think "sync" for synchronous which means the class is in real time.

Synchronous can occur in person or virtually. Whereas asynchronous is on your own time. I chose hybrid because it was suitable, once again, for my lifestyle as a wife, mother, and full-time worker. Your learning style also has a lot to do with the type of environment you thrive in. If you are not familiar with your learning style, I suggest you take a learning style assessment. This information can also help you understand the type of learning manipulatives would enhance your learning experience.

Pros and cons of attending online school only. The pros are you have flexibility. The cons are that it is a lonely journey without community. Also, you are missing out on a network after graduation. Networks are great for consultations in practice.

Again, the NP program is rigorous meaning there is a lot of in-depth information that you need to retain that will be accessed again over time. Therefore, you want to select the best learning environment for success. That's where NP Student® comes in.

Expenses (Cost)

It is a great misconception that you must break the bank to receive quality education. Please note that top performing schools can be affordable. Affordability may be a priority for an applicant who plans to pay out of pocket or just a personal preference. Historically, inflation influences the increase in the cost of tuition for graduate or doctorate education. First, cost is determined by many factors such as whether the school is private or public, notoriety, the program type (masters or doctorate) or specialty offered (FNP, AGNP, WHNP, etc.) and program resources and unique services. Proprietary schools or private schools that are for profit can be costly and not offer services that enhance the quality of your education.

When it comes to calculating the cost, look into the amount per credit hour. Credit hour is the measurement of the hours you spend on your coursework per week. It corresponds with the calendar (quarter or semester) system for that institution. Credit hours are higher for part-time than it is for full-time status. Residency is another factor that determines credit hours. If you are attending a program out of state, the credit hours are more than it would be if you were to attend in state. Some reasons students choose to attend school out of state instead of in-state schools include a waiting list, they want to attend in person or prefer to move to another state for a change.

Earlier we talked about how to pay for school. As mentioned, in the previous chapter, it is not the expected cost or fees that gets you but the unexpected costs. One year, we, NP Student® Magazine, did a feature on the unexpected costs after graduation to fully transition into the workplace. Students were surprised by the list of small things they would have never considered. Don't be surprised by the cost. Lastly note there is a cost to apply. This would include your application fee, GRE test registration fee, transcripts from all colleges attended. Get to know how much your program will cost and inquire about the little expenses that add up to be much before you determine if you can afford attending.

Before you choose an NP program, it's essential to consider the costs. In **Table 3**, I've outlined a simple way for you to break down your semester-by-semester expenses for your prospective NP programs. Use this table for each school you're considering to gain a better understanding of the financial commitment involved. Keep updating the table as you go through this chapter, so you'll have all the information you need to make your final choice.

Table 3. Semester-by-Semester Expense Breakdown for Prospective NP Programs

NP Program Name	Tuition per Semester	Fees per Semester	Estimated Book Cost	Estimated Living Expenses	Financial Aid/ Scholarships Available	Total Cost per Semester
Sample	$10,000	$500	$300	$8,000	Yes	$18,800
School 1						
School 2						
School 3						
School 4						
School 5						

Nurse Practitioner Specialties

There are eight nurse practitioner specialties that require you to sit for a national certification exam.[12] These specialties all start off with the same foundational courses and branch off into specialized courses after the second or third semester. The eight specialties are Acute Care Nurse Practitioner (ACNP), Adult-gerontology Nurse Practitioner (AGNP), Family Nurse Practitioner (FNP), Neonatal Nurse Practitioner (NNP), Oncology Nurse Practitioner (ONP), Pediatric Nurse Practitioner (PNP), Psychiatric Mental Health Nurse Practitioner (PMHNP), and Women's Health Nurse Practitioner (WHNP). Notice how they all match their corresponding population. This means that your prospective school would more than likely require you to have RN experience in the population you plan to specialize in as an NP. Therefore, understanding the pros and cons of each specialty, the job outlook (forecast of opportunities in the next 10 years), and compensation after graduation before you apply can save you time and money in the end.[14,15]

Acute Care Nurse Practitioner (ACNP)[12]

An acute care nurse practitioner specializes in providing advanced healthcare at a hospital (acute care setting). They care for patients with severe medical conditions. These conditions are often characterized by rapidly changing health needs, and management of multiple comorbidities. ACNPs also utilize their expertise to coordinate patient care, conduct comprehensive health assessments, order essential diagnostic tests, and prescribe medications. They are trained to thrive in fast-paced environments such as emergency rooms (ER) and intensive care units (ICU), where their skills ensure that patients receive timely and responsive care.

Pros: ACNPs, including those specializing in pediatric acute care, are in high demand due to their specialized skills in managing critical health situations. They are well-positioned for top-tier leadership roles such as Hospitalists, Quality and Compliance Officer or Chief Nursing Officer, where they can significantly influence patient care and hospital policies.

Cons: When you work as an ACNP, you are confined to specialized roles, which limits moving into broader areas like primary care. Additionally, the high-stress environment of hospital work can significantly strain their emotional and physical health, elevating the risk of experiencing burnout.

Job Outlook: Their sought-after skills are evident in diverse listings on job sites like Indeed, Nurse Recruiter, Monster, eNPNetwork, and LinkedIn. The 2022 AANP Nurse Practitioner Practice report indicates that 2.8% of NPs are certified in Acute Care, including 0.6% in Pediatric-Acute

Care and 5.3% in Adult-Gerontology Acute Care, highlighting expanding opportunities in this specialized field across various areas and settings.

Compensation: Nurse Practitioners, including ACNPs,, are among the higher-earning healthcare professionals. In 2022, the U.S. Bureau of Labor Statistics reported that the highest paying states for nurse practitioners overall were California ($158,130), New Jersey ($143,250), and Massachusetts ($138,700), with the lowest being Tennessee ($99,330), Alabama ($106,610), and West Virginia ($106,790). The national mean annual wage for nurse practitioners was $124,680 as of May 2022, substantially above the U.S. average wage of $61,900. For more specific salary data related to Acute Care Nurse Practitioners, resources such as Salary.com and Indeed offer insights, though these may vary in accuracy compared to BLS data.

Adult-Gerontology Nurse Practitioner (AGNP)[12,13,14,15]

Gerontology Nurse Practitioner (GNP) programs began in the 1970s and 1980s due to a growing elderly population's healthcare needs.[15,16] In 2015, they transformed into Adult-Gerontology Nurse Practitioner (AGNP) programs to better serve the aging population. Today, AGNPs play a central role in providing comprehensive care spanning from adolescents to older adults. This includes performing health assessments, diagnosing and treating various medical conditions, prescribing medications, and actively promoting overall wellness throughout an individual's lifespan.

Pros: As the population ages, AGNPs find themselves indispensable in the healthcare ecosystem. They offer specialized care for older adults, making them an integral part of the geriatric healthcare team.

Cons: The emotional toll of managing chronic illness and end-of-life care could be challenging.

Job Outlook: Growth is faster than the average for this role, signaling ample opportunities for career advancement.

Compensation: Median salaries tend to be competitive, often hovering around the $110,000 mark, depending on the state and facility.

Family Nurse Practitioner (FNP)[12,13]

A Family NP or FNP specializes in primary care from birth to senescence. FNPs practice includes preventative care, disease education and management, and health promotion.

Pros: FNPs are in demand to close the primary care provider shortage gap. FNPs also have the option to practice in general areas such as cardiology, urology, orthopedics, and aesthetics. The areas utilize assessment as foundational to care.

Cons: Today, employers are more intentional about their research when it comes to NP qualifications. For instance, a practice that provides women's health services is more likely to hire a WHNP than an FNP. Having a certification in the area you choose to practice is a plus for you and the employer. It is your responsibility to obtain special training or certifications to become qualified for a new area.

Job Outlook: Growth is faster than the average.

Compensation: The average annual salary of FNPs in the U.S. is a range from an estimated $110,000 and high of $220,000. Philadelphia reported as the highest paying city with an annual salary a little over $160,000. Whereas Alabama, Iowa, and Indiana annual FNP salaries are about

15-18% lower than the national average. The practice state, type of practice, clinical setting, cost of living, and years of experience are often the determining factors of salary. It is your responsibility to investigate the specifics before deciding where to practice as an FNP. This information can be found on Indeed.com under the "Find Salaries" section. There is a box to type in the job title, "Family Nurse Practitioner" and the desired location.

Oncology Nurse Practitioner (ONP)[12,13]

An Oncology Nurse Practitioner (ONP) specializes in the care and treatment of patients battling cancer. Operating alongside oncologists, ONPs manage symptom relief, administer therapies, and provide emotional support to patients and families. They often serve as navigators through the complicated terrain of cancer care, from diagnosis to survivorship or palliative care. Certification through the Oncology Nursing Certification Corporation (ONCC) lends an extra layer of credibility to their expertise.

Pros: You get to be part of groundbreaking research in cancer care. It's an intellectually stimulating field, often at the cutting edge of medical science.

Cons: Emotional resilience is needed, as you'll frequently engage with critically ill patients and their families.

Job Outlook: Growth is faster than the average, influenced by the increasing number of cancer cases globally.

Compensation: Generally competitive, though subject to factors like geographic location and level of expertise.

Neonatal Nurse Practitioner (NNP)[12,13]

A Neonatal Nurse Practitioner (NNP) delivers specialized care to newborns, primarily in Neonatal Intensive Care Units (NICUs). Focused on high-risk infants, NNPs collaborate with neonatologists and other healthcare professionals to offer life-sustaining treatments. Their role encompasses diagnosis, treatment, and the long-term care planning vital to these vulnerable patients. Working in environments that range from neonatal units to delivery rooms, NNPs are key players in the multidisciplinary teams that manage complex neonatal conditions.

Pros: High level of specialization and usually in high demand, particularly in hospitals with NICUs.

Cons: Stress levels are high, and the emotional toll can be challenging, given that you're dealing with the most vulnerable patient population.

Job Outlook: Growth is faster than the average, consistent with broader healthcare trends.

Compensation: Typically competitive, often exceeding the median for NPs due to the specialized nature of the work.

Pediatric Nurse Practitioner (PNP)[12,13, 18]

The Pediatric Nurse Practitioner (PNP) specializes in providing comprehensive healthcare to children, from infancy through adolescence. Established as the inaugural NP specialty by Loretta Ford and Henry Silver in 1965, PNPs diagnose, treat, and manage acute and chronic illnesses while promoting preventative care.[14] Working in settings ranging from hospitals to clinics, they collaborate with a healthcare team to deliver optimal care. For more in-depth information and resources, consider visiting the

National Association of Pediatric Nurse Practitioners website.

Pros: Opportunity to make a significant impact during the formative years of a patient's life.

Cons: Emotional challenges in dealing with sick children and concerned parents.

Job Outlook: Faster than the average growth.

Compensation: Competitive, often influenced by geographical location and specialty.

Psychiatric Mental Health Nurse Practitioner (PMHNP)[12, 13]

Psychiatric-Mental Health Nurse Practitioners (PMHNPs) are advanced practice nurses specializing in mental health care across the lifespan. They assess, diagnose, and treat mental health conditions, often in collaboration with a multidisciplinary healthcare team. Working in a range of settings from psychiatric units to community clinics, they offer both medication management and psychotherapeutic interventions. PMHNPs serve as a critical bridge in the mental health field, particularly in regions where psychiatrists are in short supply.

Pros: High demand, especially given the mental health challenges exacerbated by social trends and events like the COVID-19 pandemic.

Cons: Emotional exhaustion and 'burnout' are common, given the nature of psychiatric work.

Job Outlook: Rapid growth is expected, further emphasizing the need for mental health professionals.

Compensation: Salaries can be quite lucrative, sometimes exceeding other NP specializations.

Women's Health Nurse Practitioner (WHNP)[12, 13]

A Women's Health Nurse Practitioner (WHNP) primarily focuses on addressing women's health issues across the lifespan. Their expertise is not solely confined to reproductive and gynecological health, although these are components of their practice. WHNPs are adept at preventive care, early diagnosis, and management of conditions as varied as menstrual disorders, infertility, pre- and post-natal care, menopausal symptoms, and even gender-specific issues like breast cancer and osteoporosis.

Pros: Specialized focus allows for a deep understanding of women's health issues, from adolescence through senescence.

Cons: Limited to women's health, thus less versatile compared to FNPs.

Job Outlook: Growth is faster than the average, reflecting the broader trends in healthcare.

Compensation: Competitive, though specialization might offer additional opportunities for higher compensation.

Even more, specialties differ from area and settings. For instance, I worked in the urgent care at a men's jail. My specialty is FNP, and I worked in an urgent care setting in corrections. I would not have been qualified for this position as a WHNP. Another example of working in an alternate setting is when I worked at the student health care center on a college campus. I would not have been qualified for this role as an NNP. In other words, if you desire to work in an alternate area, consider pursuing the FNP track because it focuses on general health, and you are in a better position to build upon your assessment foundation.

I also understand there is a primary care provider shortage, and you may be pressured by family members or a mentor to pursue this area. However, primary care or family practice is not for everyone. The same way the acute care setting was not for me as an RN. If you are undecided about the track, becoming an FNP allows you to branch into other fields and have flexibility in the workplace, and you can always return to your school to obtain a certificate in another specialty. Keep in mind that you can work in a specialty of your specialty. For instance, FNPs working in aesthetics, dermatology, orthopedics, and home health are not uncommon. This fact is what accounts for the versatility of this profession which makes it attractive to many.

When it comes to selecting a specialty, start with the population that interests you the most or the population that corresponds with the area you work in now. For instance, if your experience is rooted in the Medical-Surgical (Med-Surg) unit of a children's hospital, a Pediatric Nurse Practitioner role may be a logical progression for you.

Understanding the DNP degree in NP Education

As an NP student at Brenau, I remember them encouraging us to return for our DNP after graduation. Mainly, the National Organization of Nurse Practitioner Faculties (NONPF) endorsed the Doctor of Nursing Practice (DNP) as the entry-level qualification for Nurse Practitioners by 2015.[19] Their goal was to elevate practice standards, address complex healthcare challenges, and enhance leadership and evidence-based practice within the nursing profession. 'Doctor Nurse? Why not just attend medical school?' was my initial reaction, as I did not fully understand the degree's value. In addition, many employers back then did not offer additional compensation for the DNP, possibly due to a similar lack of understanding. This left me questioning whether to include this historical context. However, NONPF released an updated statement once again endorsing the upcoming transition of MSN NP to DNP NP as the point of entry for nurse practitioners by 2025.[20] Therefore, I will share my experience briefly because the DNP degree is something to at least consider before you apply.

As outlined in **Table 1**, a DNP is a practice-focused terminal nursing degree, in contrast to a Doctor of Philosophy (PhD), which is research-based. Put simply, a DNP focuses on outcomes, while a PhD centers on findings. There are two main tracks: post-baccalaureate (BSN to DNP) and post-masters (MSN to DNP). I chose the post-master's track three years after NP school, having gained sufficient clinical practice experience to easily identify gaps for my scholarly project. Such projects, also known as DNP, quality improvement, or capstone projects, are designed to evaluate processes and outcomes to guide practice and policy. They lay a foundation for future practice scholarship.

Even if I knew then what I know now, I wouldn't have chosen the BSN to DNP track. Clinical practice experience before the DNP provides deeper insights and better positions one to effect change. Alternatively, I've observed that students who go straight from BSN to DNP often lack the interest or time to apply their RN practice improvements post-DNP, mainly due to the transition to NP clinical practice. Deciding whether to go for a DNP right after your baccalaureate or after gaining some NP experience has its own set of pros and cons. It all comes down to whether you want to dive straight into it or gain some real-world experience first.

Understanding the DNP degree is necessary, especially given the evolving direction of NP education. Today, I recognize the immense value of holding a DNP degree. For instance, it removed the cap on my compensation, positioning me as an expert qualified for a variety of unlisted employment opportunities.

With a DNP, you can serve as a consultant, contribute to hospital or institutional boards, and significantly influence changes that benefit the nursing profession. Moreover, it equips you with the expertise to identify and solve practice gaps, possibly even leading to starting your own business as a solution. A DNP is not a boost for you, it is a chance to make a real impact in policy as well as practice.

Here are two more dimensions to consider:

How NP Practice Has Changed: The healthcare landscape is in constant flux, influenced by demographic shifts, policy changes, and technological advances. For NPs, this has led to expanded roles, increased autonomy, and the requirement for broader skill sets. What remains static today may evolve tomorrow. Thus, your ability to adapt is not just an asset; it's a necessity.

Non-Traditional NP Positions and Their Relevance: Beyond hospital and clinical settings, NPs are finding roles in policy advocacy, telehealth, and academic research. As the definition of healthcare broadens, so do the avenues for professional application of your skills. Being aware of these non-traditional paths isn't merely beneficial; it's imperative to make an informed decision about your specialization.

So, when you're thinking about these different roles and their specific needs, ask yourself: Are you picking a focus just based on what's happening today or are you thinking about how you'll fit into the future of healthcare? Your choice will reflect not just your current skill set but the scope of your ambition and the depth of your commitment to fostering equitable, quality healthcare.

Program of Study

The program of study is the curriculum plan that your NP degree will follow for conferral. It coincides with your enrollment status. For instance, if you are a part-time student, your curriculum plan will be extended throughout the more semesters than a full-time student. All NP curricula start with foundational courses including nursing theory, health policy, nursing research, thesis or project writing, role development, advanced pathophysiology, and advanced health physical assessment, and advanced pharmacology. Pay attention to if your course is online or in person if you plan to attend a hybrid program. Matriculation is very similar to that of your undergraduate program. You cannot advance to the next course until the foundational courses are complete. Last, your major courses are associated with the specialty that you choose.

For International Students

Some schools require students to verify their citizenship. For this reason, it is important to mention that the application process for international students who obtained their nursing degree from abroad has additional steps to vet the coursework. Therefore, these prospects must provide an evaluation from the Commission on Graduates of Foreign Nursing Schools.[21] Be sure to check with the school for their policy on entering with a non-nursing degree as well as the requirements for English as a second language. Some schools may require you to take the Test of English as a Foreign Language (TOEFL), International English Language Testing System (IELTS), or Duolingo test.

Enrollment

Everything we have discussed thus far leads up to becoming enrolled into a program. Things to look for when you are checking out enrollment. What is the acceptance rate? What is the average class or cohort size? How often do they accept students per year? When you compare the number of students enrolled to the graduation rate, it tells you a lot about their students' completion rate.

I would also inquire about what support services they provide to help students navigate through academic and life challenges. We will discuss the different emerging support services that exist in Chapter 5. During my first semester of DNP school, my grandmother in-law and cousin passed two weeks apart. The next semester my son was hospitalized for one week. A week after he was discharged, I was in a rear end collision where I sustained a concussion. At this point, I thought all signs were pointing to "quit the program." I shared my concerns with the coordinator who later spoke with the Associate Dean with the program to come up with a solution to keep me in the program. After all, I was performing well grade wise. They worked with me until I recovered, and I was able to graduate on time. Where am I going? A school that has student support services is concerned about their students' success. It is a risk attending a school that handles life challenges on a case-by-case basis. Trust me, your life could be perfect at the beginning of the program and havoc hits the second to the last semester of school. Set yourself up for success by taking interest in the support services.

Advanced training and specialized options

Graduate reviews are a solid source to learn about past students' experiences from application to graduation. Many of you may already have a school in mind because you were referred by a former student. Past students can authentically comment on the ease of the program which includes the structure and function of the program including their interactions with faculty. They also can be a preceptor source. In fact, some programs have incorporated a preceptor exchange program where former students share their contact with the current students.

The job placement rate is another important metric. After all, the ultimate goal of undergoing extensive education is to secure employment shortly after graduation. Some institutions are known for the high caliber of professionals they produce. Again, the U.S. News and World Report name NPs as the best health care job in 2024 which is a promising statistic.[22] However, one should never assume they will not encounter barriers with landing a job. It's essential to consult reliable sources such as the U.S. BLS for job outlook data, which we have touched upon in the section on NP specialties. Secondly, it depends on how prospects market themselves. Furthermore, the job placement rate could reflect the geographical location or the school's reputation. This rate may not be readily available on the website. There, you would have to inquire during a tour or call the admissions counselor. If the admissions' counselor does not have this information on hand, ask them to inquire from the graduate program director or an equivalent. Every school should know their job placement rate for each graduating class. If not, consider other institutions that value this data.

Despite what many may believe, patients are increasingly discerning about their healthcare providers. They often want to know where you received your training and how long you've been practicing, as this information engenders a sense of trust. I view this as a positive indicator of a patient's desire to establish a rapport and become more involved in their care. One could also translate this as patients being more involved in their care when they are comfortable.

Additionally, it's imperative to investigate the availability of NP residencies and fellowship programs before applying. At the time of writing, NP residencies have been around for less than 20 years, with the first program established in 2007 by the Community Health Center, Inc. in Connecticut. The rise of these residencies has been significantly influenced by the primary care shortage and the expanding aging population. If you seek a guided transition from graduation to practice, especially in specialized settings, a residency could offer this bridge.

Think of these programs as an extended learning opportunity where you get paid. Fellowships, which may entail additional fees, provide specialized, focused training. Residency and fellowships have many benefits, one is ameliorating the transition to practice for new graduates. I applied to one of the earliest primary care residencies a year after completing my NP program, an experience I will discuss more about in the next book. As of now, my alma mater has partnered with Carl Vinson Veteran Affairs Medical Center to offer a primary care residency program.[23]

I was pleased with the quality of education I received from my program, at least in theory. The class size was small, and the hybrid format suited my personality type well. I enjoyed the in-person interactions because I'm a sociable person, while also appreciating the flexibility of completing assignments online to be available for my family. One of my colleagues exited the program to pursue a career as a physician, making that decision in the first semester. She confided that she was not satisfied with the program's educational level and harbored higher aspirations. I encouraged her to follow her passion, and today she is a general surgeon. My point is, if you yearn for a more advanced level of education, it is entirely acceptable to consider medical school. Ultimately, conducting thorough research for NP school can guide you in making an informed decision about your preferred path.

Dr. Little's Prescription:

Refer to **Table 4** as a template, then use it to fill out the comparison chart in **Table 5** for your top three to five preferred schools. Be sure to attend an interest meeting or Q&A session for those top choices before you attend. If the school you are interested in does not offer an interesting meeting, do your best to schedule a visit to tour your future school.

Table 4. Sample Comparison Chart for Top Nurse Practitioner Schools

Criteria	School 1	School 2	School 3
Location	Atlanta, GA	Chicago, IL	Boston, MA
Accreditation	CCNE	ACEN	ACEN
Program Length	24 months	26 months	28 months
Tuition (Annual)	$25,000	$30,000	$35,000
Clinical Hours Required	600	750	650
Specialization Options	Family, Psychiatry	Adult-Gerontology, Pediatric	Acute Care, Psychiatric
Interest Meeting Held?	Yes, monthly	Yes, quarterly	Yes, twice a year
Faculty Credentials	80% DNP, 20% PhD	50% DNP, 50% PhD	75% DNP, 25% PhD
Research Opportunities	Yes, robust	Limited	Extensive
Global Perspective	Offers international clinical experience	None	Limited

Table 5. Blank Comparison Chart for Top Nurse Practitioner Schools

Criteria School's Name	School 1:	School 2:	School 3:
Location			
Accreditation			
Program Length			
Tuition (Annual)			
Clinical Hours Required			
Specialization Options			
Interest Meeting Held?			
Faculty Credentials			
Research Opportunities			
Global Perspective			

Chapter 3
Becoming the Ideal Candidate

Don't just stand out on paper, stand out as a person.

Key Points
- A good GPA and RN experience are not enough to get accepted into a competitive program.
- Your personal statement conveys your authenticity.
- Building professional relationships lead to strong recommendations.
- Early submission applicants stand out from the rest by promptly meeting admission requirements.

As we take this next step towards becoming a nurse practitioner, It is also important to mention that the ideal candidate goes beyond traditional norms and physical abilities. In this inclusive and progressive era, the ideal nurse practitioner candidate is not just defined by traditional norms but by a rich blend of empathy, diverse life experiences, and the ability to connect with patients from all walks of life. This includes nurses with disabilities, racial and cultural backgrounds, genders, and sexual orientations. The field recognizes that such diversity enriches the profession, leading to a more qualified, inclusive, and equitable healthcare practice.

NP school admissions can be competitive especially at a renowned institution that attracts a high volume of applicants. For this reason, these schools employ rigorous screening processes to identify candidates who mirror their ideal student profiles. Therefore, strategically positioning yourself to match the caliber of student the school wants, can increase your chance of being selected. This entails thinking like an NP even before you become one. For instance, consider how you currently educate patients and plan their follow-up care. Now ask yourself, 'If I were already an NP, how would my approach differ?

It is also important to mention that today's ideal candidate is not defined solely by physical ability or traditional norms. In this inclusive and progressive era, the ideal candidate embodies a blend of empathy, diverse life experiences, and the ability to connect with patients from all walks of life. Today's highly qualified NP candidate encompasses much more than traditional criteria. This includes individuals with disabilities, people from a variety of racial and cultural backgrounds, and those of different genders and sexual orientations. The field recognizes that such diversity enriches the profession, leading to a more qualified, inclusive, and effective healthcare practice.

Imagine yourself in your desired specialized nursing role, gaining invaluable experience and insight into the day-to-day responsibilities. This mental exercise of visualizing yourself in your specialty is not just about developing skills;

it is an intentional step towards establishing your professional profile. As you move from visualization to attending NP school, you will get more exposure and your name could come up as a prospective candidate for job opportunity discussions. Could that be you?

To answer this, let us first break down the essential attributes that can position you as the ideal candidate for a competitive NP program. We will start by comparing two highly qualified candidates.

While impeccable RN experience, credentials, and test scores may seem like a guaranteed path to acceptance, it's imperative to understand that these attributes alone do not secure your seat. Let's consider an example. Imagine two candidates: Amina and Sarah. Both have high GPAs, compelling personal statements, and extensive clinical experience. They've also graduated from top-tier schools, making them ostensibly well-qualified. Amina has three years of RN clinical experience primarily in pediatric oncology, where she's honed her skills in patient care, family education, and treatment coordination. Sarah, on the other hand, brings three years of diversified RN clinical experience with a focus on critical care in an ICU setting, offering her a broad perspective on acute medical conditions and patient management.

However, Sarah is an average candidate who excels primarily on paper. On the other hand, Amina's GRE scores were around the 50th percentile, lower than the ideal range. However, she embodies the ideal candidate because she also demonstrates exceptional soft skills such as emotional intelligence, teamwork, and problem-solving. If you were a recruiter, who would you choose? This hypothetical scenario offers a glimpse into the mindset of admission officers, emphasizing the importance of standing out not just on paper, but as a well-rounded individual. Soft skills do matter, and I want you to be fully prepared for this multifaceted evaluation.

Take a look at **Table 6** to understand what admissions committees are looking for. This table shows that being a great candidate is about more than just grades and experience. By aiming for the qualities listed in **Table 6**, you'll be setting yourself up for a successful career as an NP.

Table 6. Comparative Attributes of Average vs. Ideal Candidates for Nurse Practitioner Programs

Attributes	Ideal Candidate	Average Candidate
Academic Credentials	3.75	3.75
Clinical Experience	Three years of ICU clinical experience with diverse clinical experience with a focus in the desired specialization	Three years of RN clinical experience with diverse clinical experience with a focus in the desired specialization
GRE Scores	Verbal: 162, Quantitative: 164, Writing: 5.0	Verbal: 162, Quantitative: 160, Writing: 4.5
Personal statement	Compelling	Compelling
Leadership experience	Serves as a charge nurse, actively participates in the Quality Improvement Committee, and has spearheaded a patient-care initiative adopted hospital-wide.	Regular RN duties without additional roles like charge nurse or committee member.
Responsiveness to Program Correspondence	Responds within one to two days of correspondence to the program.	Responds in two weeks of correspondence to the program.
Professionalism	Cooperative with requests and arrives to interview early, well-prepared, courteous.	On-time but minimally prepared and occasionally tries to talk her way out of some requests.
Adaptability	Exceptional	Average

Prerequisites and Transcripts

An official copy of your transcripts to verify your prerequisites, grade point average (GPA) degree is also required.[1] An official transcript contains your academic history at your current or past schools. It is usually secured with a seal and signature. There are three ways you can obtain a copy for a fee. You can order directly from the registrar's office, via your student account, or through a third-party company that houses transcripts. It is important that you plan when ordering a copy to accompany your application because the processing time may be different for each institution. First make a list of every school you attended, especially the ones where you took your prerequisites. Then gather the addresses of each school you plan to attend to place on your order.

A few exceptions to meeting your school's prerequisite is a course that is over ten years old and when you are actively enrolled in a BSN program. If you are still enrolled in your BSN program, you can request a copy which will show that you are actively enrolled. Some schools will make an exception and accept an unofficial copy. Be sure to contact the register office for their transcript policy. You can also contact your state's Regents for higher education to assist you with locating your transcript. In general, it is a good practice to keep an official copy or two of your transcripts for your personal records.

Resume and Curriculum Vitae (CV)

Most schools request a resume or curriculum vitae (CV) as part of the application. These documents should encapsulate your education, work experience, professional development, community and volunteer activities, as well as any research and publications. The primary distinction between a resume and a CV lies in the scope and detail. A resume is often a concise, one-to-two-page summary of your professional history tailored to the specific role. On the other hand, your CV serves as a comprehensive record of your academic and professional trajectory, including awards, certifications, publications, and accomplishments.

Now it's time to level up your RN resume to highlight your experiences and skills that will make you stand out as an ideal candidate for a NP program. Refining your resume involves more than just a surface-level update. It's an opportunity to strategically emphasize experiences and skills that resonate with the NP role. Why settle for a basic resume when you can create one that stands out and fits your career goals? Make time to revisit each section of your resume, from education and work experience to professional development and volunteer activities. Highlight responsibilities and achievements that directly relate to nursing practice and patient care, especially in areas that you aim to specialize in as an NP. If you're targeting a program or institution that leverages digital platforms for their application process, ensure your resume is optimized for readability on all devices including and tablets.

Crafting Your Personal Statement

The other component of your application is your personal statement which is also known as your admissions cover letter for some schools. It is the first introduction to you and should be impressive and well thought out. The faculty are seeking to grasp your personality, your ability to express your thoughts, to understand why you are pursuing an NP degree, and why you want to attend their program in a short moment. Crafting a personal statement can be intimidating and I often encourage my students to be authentic to make their essay memorable. Although, your personal statement is personal. Avoid using the same personal statement from your undergraduate application. Mainly, your new personal statement should reflect your growth including professional accomplishments as well as a new set of career goals.

Before getting started ask yourself the following questions:

- What is unique about me that I bring to advanced practice nursing?
- What's the story behind me wanting to become an NP? Who or what event inspired me to pursue an NP degree?
- What are my core values?
- What clinical experience do I have to assure that I'm NP a good fit?
- What kind of innovative projects or activities have I done at work that brought about change?
- Do I have any discrepancies in my GRE score or transcripts?
- Why do I want to attend this school? What makes it unique from the others I have reviewed?

Personal Statement Do's

- Be sure to know the word count. The average length for most personal statements is between 500 and 1000.
- Verify if you are free writing or responding to a question provided by your school. You do not have to wait until you are ready to apply to get started.
- You can begin your draft today, revisit and edit in the future. Invest in an editor or have a friend with exceptional editing skills proofread your statement.
- Do mention the core values of the school that aligns with yours as well as your personal mission statement.

Here is a standard personal statement outline you can follow when a writing prompt is not provided.

1. **Opening statement:** Captivate your readers (the NP admissions committee) with a compelling introduction that sets the tone for your essay.

2. **Supportive Point #1:** Discuss one reason why you are a good fit.
3. **Supportive Point #2:** Share another reason you're qualified.
4. **Supportive Point #3:** Add one more key argument or example.
5. **Conclusion statement:** Here is where you restate a line from your opening statement and summarize the points made in the meat of your essay.

Personal Statement Don'ts

You're welcome to include other relevant information you feel would add value to your personal statement. It is safe to mention one unusual hardship, the steps you took to navigate it, and transcend at work. However, I would stay clear of a laundry list of challenges you had to overcome or anything that would predict your acceptance would come with tests and trials. Please note there is an exception for candidates with disabilities.

Students with Disabilities

RNs with a disability can also become NPs. Many educational institutions and healthcare employers now offer reasonable accommodations to make this transition possible. If you face mental or physical challenges that may affect your application process, proactively communicate with the admissions department; they are often well-equipped to facilitate appropriate accommodations. Remember, your unique perspective adds value to diversity, equity, and inclusion (DEI) initiatives within the healthcare workforce.

For additional support, consider reaching out to advocacy organizations such as the National Organization of Nurses with Disabilities (NOND).[2] These groups can provide not just emotional support but also practical resources and guidance to help navigate the educational and professional landscape.

Writing Sample

Some schools may require a writing sample or supplemental writing as part of the admission process. This is where you will have the opportunity to demonstrate your academic or scholarly writing skills using the American Psychological Association (APA) format. If you are an RN with a Bachelor of Science in Nursing (BSN), you have used this format in your nursing research class.

To my ADNs and teens, nursing research is an essential part of nursing theory and an early introduction to evidence-based practices or how nursing science informs practice. Typically, it is completed in the second year of most BSN tracks. Students are expected to apply in a research paper. As a part of most graduate programs, NP students should expect to do a capstone project or research paper. Therefore, a sample writing provides a baseline and predicts if you can keep up with the theoretical portion of the graduate work, not just the practical or clinical part.

If academic writing intimidates you, don't worry. You are connected to the right source. I've not only honed my writing capabilities in the nursing realm but have also disseminated my knowledge through scholarly publications. I've included a link to writing resources that have served me well throughout my academic journey. Remember, you are connected to the right source. Not only have I mastered writing in nursing, but I've also been able to disseminate through publication. I've placed a link to writing resources that I invested in as an undergraduate nursing student and continue to use along my journey as an expert. These tools allowed me to focus on my creativity as a writer and ensured the precision of my citation formatting.

When it comes to submitting your writing sample, schools generally employ one of three approaches. First, they requested it as a standard part of the application. The other approach is the admission counselor, dean or a designated faculty member will reach out and ask you to submit a sample. Be sure to be clear on the word count and deadline of this assignment. You would not want to miss out on your acceptance because you did not keep up with the timeline. After all, the fact that they ask for a sample writing means you're one step closer to being accepted. Lastly, some schools conduct an interview and subsequently direct you to a computer where you will be given a writing prompt. Expect approximately 45 minutes to complete this assignment, adhering to APA format. In my experience, I was required to submit writing samples during my applications to both NP and DNP programs.

Preparing for the Graduate Record Examination (GRE)

The time it takes to prepare the GRE can be gruesome. Therefore, verify if a GRE score is required for admissions before adjusting your schedule. After all, scheduling is a major component of NP Student life and practice.

Here's how you can prepare for the test:

1. Take a practice test to serve as a diagnostic to get your baseline in the verbal, math, and writing sections.
2. Make a study plan using resources such as Educational Testing Service (ETS), Kaplan, or Princeton Review. Please note that these organizations also offer free test prep materials to get started.
3. Practice the test again and again until you achieve the score that is required. If you are still having

challenges, you can take a review course or hire a private GRE tutor.
4. Obtain the school codes for each prospective school. This ensures that your scores are sent to the correct institutions, a seemingly minor detail that holds significant implications.
5. As your test date approaches, invest time in fine-tuning your strategies, reviewing problem areas, and engaging in mental and emotional preparation.

Securing Strong Recommendations

Most programs require two or three recommendation letters as a part of your application. In general, your recommendation letter should be completed by individuals who have observed your nursing skills, are familiar with your knowledge, and abilities in the past 10 years. These Individuals or references would include a former nursing faculty member, mentor, preceptor, or supervisor.

Some schools provide a recommendation form to be completed by your reference. While other schools may ask you to provide your reference's name and current email address to email them a secured link to complete a recommendation form. Either way, make it an appointment to know the method your prospective school uses.

Start reaching out to your mentor, supervisor, and former instructors to share your professional goals as soon as you decide to apply. Be sure to ask them if they would support your next steps by writing a letter of recommendation. It is important to ask because for whatever reason some individuals may not want to support you the next time.

If you do not have any professional relationships, you can join a local chapter of a national association, your state's nursing organization or even volunteer at a local clinic that employs nurse practitioners. Be sure to maintain and cultivate the relationships and not just use them solely for recommendations. It is your responsibility to make a good impression. Building professional relationships is a practice you continue throughout your entire career.

Maintaining Your Professional Image

Another thing you want to watch is your social media. Another thing you want to watch is your social media. Social media accounts link back to you even if you use another alias. Your posts can be traced back to your followers who use their real name who like your posts and vice versa. The point is you want to always keep it professional.

Invest in a photographer for a professional profile headshot or do it yourself (DIY) until you are able to invest in one.[3,4] Your professionalism doesn't begin at the start of the program, it begins now. People are watching. In the words of Kim Kardashian, be cognizant because "the camera is always rolling." Establishing a professional profile helps you stand out to recruiters who do a social media sweep before selecting candidates for the interview process.

It's Never Too Early

Being proactive and submitting admission requirements early also sets you apart from the other applicants. This paperwork includes a copy of your Basic Life Support (BLS) for providers cardiopulmonary resuscitation (CPR) certification, a copy of your immunization record, immunization exemption or vaccination waiver form for two Measles Mumps and Rubella (MMR) doses, three Hepatitis B doses, documented history of chicken pox or two varicella doses, and one dose of tetanus Diphtheria and pertussis (TDAP). A purified protein derivative (PPD) test or They were required for clinicals in undergrad as well.

Financial preparation extends beyond tuition and books; it includes essential clinical attire and equipment as well. Once your paperwork gains approval, your school will guide you on when and where to purchase items like your white lab coat and personalized, engraved name badge. Typically, clinicals do not start until the second or third semester depending on the matriculation plan. Prepare to invest in a good pair of non-slip shoes, compression socks, a monitoring stethoscope, and more. Much like a proficient nurse practitioner anticipates the next steps in patient care, you too should plan for your clinical needs. Use **Table 7** as a standard shopping list to gather all the essential apparel and supplies you'll need for your first day of clinicals. Additional space is included for any miscellaneous items that may either enhance your clinical experience or are mandated by your program.

Table 7. Clinical Essentials Checklist

Clinical Essentials Checklist	
ITEM	Price
School Name Badge	
Non-slip Shoes	
Compression Socks	
Stethoscope	
Clinical Notebook	
Clinical Bag	
Clinical Supplies (pen lights, reflex hammer, tuning fork, eye chart, and body measure tape, etc.)	
Reference books	
Student Health Insurance	
Reservation Deposit	
Practice Liability Insurance	
Total	

Dr. Little's Prescription:

Here are three things you can do to help you become an ideal candidate.

1. Secure three recommendation letters from individuals who can vouch for your clinical experience, character, and dedication.

2. Actively express gratitude to those who have contributed to your professional journey.
3. Start crafting your personal statement. Do something that enhances your relationship with your references or mentors. It is good practice to demonstrate gratitude. and begin your personal statement.

Chapter 4
Time to Apply

When in doubt, always refer to the school's website.

Key Points
- 💡 Different application cycles can be overwhelming, and securing admission may not be straightforward for each NP school.
- 💡 Using NursingCAS streamlines the application process to multiple NP schools.
- 💡 Disclosure on applications ensures integrity, avoids delays, and prevents rejection.

Now it's time to put the pieces together and apply. The application cycle can vary from regular to rolling. In a regular admissions cycle, there's a set timeline for the nursing school staff to collect applications, review them, and respond to candidates. Rolling admissions, conversely, means that applications are reviewed by staff as they are received. For example, if you are aiming to start your program in the fall of August, your application could be due as early as the previous November or as late as February of the current year. It is important to familiarize yourself with the application window for each prospective school well before you apply. Another option to consider is early decision, which may require you to apply up to a year in advance, depending on the school's calendar.

Step One: Choose Your Top Schools

In **Chapter 2**, you completed a comparison chart of potential schools. The time has now come to narrow that list to two or three top schools. This step serves as the linchpin for your subsequent application strategy, setting the stage for a more targeted and effective approach.

Step Two: Gather Your Documents

It is good practice to have a folder with all the documents that support your application. We discussed several in the last chapter. Additional documents include a copy of your unencumbered nursing license and certifications, evidence of your RN clinical experience, and perhaps your writing sample.

Step Three: Creating an Account

It is important to review each prospective school's website in its entirety since the NP School application process is not standardized. For instance, the school's landing page may have application prompts that say "apply, apply here, apply now, or learn more." Sometimes it is located under "graduate programs" or program" The next step is to create an account. If you obtained your undergraduate degree at that school, then select "returning user."

If you have challenges recalling the email you used, call the registrar's office to obtain the correct email. Be ready to provide your student ID. Next, request a new password because chances are if you forgot the email address you may have forgotten the password too. If that email account is closed, then create a new account to avoid spending unnecessary energy on something trivial.

When it comes to the email you use as your default contact for the application, be sure you check spam at the beginning and that you have a quick response time too. More than likely you will receive a verification email to confirm your email. Therefore, cooking your evening dinner is not an activity to do while creating your account because the verification email may be time sensitive. Once you confirm your email, you may be prompted to create a password. This is a good time to write your password in your journal to refer to later. The next prompt will be to "start a new application," "start your application," or "create an application."

Nursing Centralized Application Service (CAS), provided by the American Association of Colleges of Nursing (AACN), streamlines the process of applying to nursing programs at various levels, including associate, baccalaureate, master's, and doctoral degrees. It simplifies the application process by allowing you to understand the admissions requirements, upload necessary documents, and submit your transcripts through one platform.

Step Four: Submit Your Application

You are in the application, you have your documents, and now are ready to enter your information. Submitting your application is the well anticipated step you have been waiting for and should be straightforward at this point. In general, there is a section for your enrollment information (program of choice, education history with the school, affiliation with the U.S. military, and at times referral), demographics or personal information, academic history.

There is also a disclosure section on your background information which includes history of suspension, expulsion, dismissal or probation from a high school, college, or university. This section also inquires about any history of convictions, pleas or contest to a felony or misdemeanor. The next two sections outline how to address these special considerations to ensure application integrity, avoid delays, and prevent rejection.

Addressing Suspension or Probation in High School or College*

Honesty and Disclosure: Begin by being transparent. Most applications include a section asking about disciplinary history. A good practice is to disclose this information honestly, as failure to do so can lead to more severe consequences.

Contextualize the Incident: Briefly describe the circumstances that led to the suspension or probation. Avoid overly detailed explanations or justifications. The goal is to provide context, not excuses.

Reflect on the Learning Experience: This is where you turn a negative into a positive. Discuss what you learned from the experience and how it contributed to your personal growth. For instance, "This experience taught me the importance of accountability and integrity, which are vital in the nursing profession."

Evidence of Change: Provide examples of how you've changed since the incident. This could include positive behaviors, community service, or other constructive activities that demonstrate your commitment to personal growth and professional ethics.

Recommendations and Support: If applicable, include references or recommendations from individuals who can vouch for your character and development since the incident.

Some applications are very lengthy. Therefore, save your application if you need to take a break. The status should say, "In progress," and when you log back in it should say, "continue application" or something similar.

NP School Application Etiquette

1. Apply to the correct program and specialty.
2. Write, "Not applicable" in areas where a response is needed to complete the application but does not apply.
3. Upload your edited personal statement.
4. Have at least two trusted friends or family members proofread your application to identify grammatical errors and to confirm your thoughts are complete.
5. Sign off on the application. This can take place just before you submit or right before you review. It's just another step to verify it is you.
6. Check for the confirmation that the application was submitted. This should pop up right after or be sent to the email account you used to set up your account.

Addressing Criminal History*

If you need to add information about a criminal conviction on your NP school application, first consult an attorney for legal advice. Then, emphasize your personal development and rehabilitation efforts, highlighting your commitment to healthcare ethics. This approach demonstrates responsibility and aligns with the principles of the nursing profession.

***Disclaimer:** Please note that the information provided here is not legal advice. It is intended for informational and educational purposes only. I strongly recommend consulting with an attorney for specific advice regarding your individual situation, particularly if it involves criminal history. My expertise lies in advanced nursing education and practice, and while I aim to offer guidance, legal matters should be addressed by a legal expert.

Dr. Little's Prescription:

Go ahead! Apply and be sure to email me when you are done at drpatrice@npstudent.com to let me know you got in.

Chapter 5
The Next Step

Your lifestyle affects how well you do in NP school.

Key Points

- Waiting can feel unproductive, but it is an opportunity for personal development.
- Rushing your decision without considering your options can lead to regret in your choice of NP school.
- Your path may require difficult decisions, like leaving a job, to fully commit to the program.

Since launching NP Student® Magazine in 2018, I have had the honor of guiding NP students from education to graduation, unraveling the complex threads of the transition. One common hurdle I've noticed is the anxiety many feel about reaching out to schools. Is this fear based on the idea that being persistent is annoying? Or does it show that soft skills like communication are getting less attention in today's world of texting and short messages?

I recall one student who, with a little guidance and encouragement, overcame this fear and found her voice. It was a transformation that went beyond academics, leading to personal and career growth.

Reflecting on the complexities faced by pre-nursing, Wynter's story stands out as a particularly inspiring example. Her journey, marked by challenges and triumphs, encapsulates the essence of transformation through dedicated mentorship.

Wynter's Story

'Over the last decade, nursing school acceptance has become much more competitive. Professional groups and hospitals are pushing for more education, correlating higher education levels in nurses with better patient care. The challenge of securing admittance into a BSN degree program today is significant. In this competitive landscape, Dr. Little's bootcamp, was instrumental in my journey to join an RN program. Dr. Little's expertise in navigating the admissions process, including essays, resumes, and prerequisites, was invaluable. Her guidance in crafting personal essays was especially critical, helping me find my voice and articulate my potential as a nurse.

The journey to becoming a nurse is arduous, often feeling like an uphill battle demanding blood, sweat, and tears. Dr. Little's support didn't cease with the arrival of my admittance letter; she continued to assist me in organizing my priorities and deadlines, and provided consistent encouragement throughout the initial challenging semester. Now, one year into my nursing program and with a graduation date set for 2020, I've secured a nursing externship at a prestigious hospital and am thriving, not just surviving.

Nursing, often cited as one of the hardest degrees to attain in America, is a path filled with doubts about one's intelligence and skill, and overwhelming course schedules. Yet, it's also a journey of incredible growth and excitement, both academically and personally. For anyone aspiring to join the nursing ranks in Georgia, I can say with absolute confidence that Dr. Patrice Little is an invaluable asset.

After finishing her nursing program, Wynter worked in the Intensive Care Unit (ICU) for two years, developing her assessment skills. She then decided to become a nurse practitioner. I was honored to write her a recommendation letter for NP school. Her progression from ICU nurse to NP student illustrates the continuous journey of growth in nursing, also highlighting the impact of hard work and persistent mentorship. Wynter's success is an example for other nursing students, showing what can be achieved with dedication and support.

Embracing the journey towards becoming an NP involves not only courage and clear communication but also patience and fortitude. As you go through applications and admissions, the waiting period is inevitable.

The Wait

The waiting phase is a period that every aspiring NP must face. This phase is filled with hope and uncertainty. While it is an inevitable part of the journey, it does not have to be spent as a time of anxiety or frustration. Instead, let's focus on a few activities that can make this time more productive and fulfilling, understanding that it is not just a pause in the process, but a vital time for preparation and growth.

There are three possible scenarios you can prepare for while you wait: an interview invitation, acceptance, or no response. As we explore strategies for this waiting period, it's important to consider these potential outcomes. This section will provide guidance on how to navigate each of these situations effectively. Whether you receive an acceptance, an interview invitation, or face a period of no response, you'll be prepared for the next steps as you embark on NP school.

Scenario 1: How to prepare for your interview

The interview is the final phase before acceptance, often serving as the final step or bridge between applicants and their acceptance. It is essential to be authentic and thoroughly familiar with your resume and personal statement. Expect questions similar to those in a job interview, including behavioral questions that assess how you respond to challenges. To prepare for this scenario:

Professional Dress: Appearance matters. Dressing professionally means choosing attire that is neat, clean, and appropriate for the interview context. Keep in mind that personal elements like tattoos, nose piercings and locs can be part of your professional image, especially when well-groomed. The key is to balance personal expression with professional appropriateness, demonstrating respect for the interview process and the potential employer.

Thank You Cards: Bring thank you cards to leave with your interviewers post-interview. This small gesture can leave a lasting, positive impression. It is also one of my secrets to standing out from other candidates. You can also send a Thank You email as provided in **Table 8.**

Copies of Documents: Always carry extra copies of your CV and personal statement. This shows preparedness and makes it easier for interviewers to reference specific parts of your qualifications and experience during the discussion.

Review Your Documents: Examine your resume and personal statements thoroughly. Be ready to discuss any points from these documents.

Practice Behavioral Responses: Reflect on and prepare your responses to potential behavioral questions based on past experiences or challenges working as an RN. If you do not have any RN experience, reflect on behavior scenarios from your RN clinicals.

Understand the Role and Institution: Gain an understanding of the school's mission and values. Revisit **Chapter 2** for more.

Prepare Your Own Questions: Be ready to ask insightful questions showing your genuine interest and engagement.

Mock Interviews: Practice interviewing to build your confidence and fine-tune your responses. Seeking feedback from friends or family for improvement.

Table 8. Post-Interview Follow-up Email

Post-Interview Follow-Up Email (to be sent within 24 hours after the interview)
Subject: Thank You for the Interview - [Your Full Name] Dear [Recipient's Name], I wanted to express my gratitude for the opportunity to interview for the Nurse Practitioner program at [University Name] on [Date of Interview]. I enjoyed our conversation and gained a deeper understanding of the program and its unique offerings. The interview reinforced my interest in your esteemed program and I am confident that my skills and aspirations would align well with your educational approach. Thank you again for your time and consideration. I look forward to the possibility of contributing to [University Name] and eagerly await any updates regarding my application status. Best regards, [Your Full Name]

Scenario 2: Acceptance and Decision Making

If you receive an acceptance letter, it's an exciting milestone in your journey. To prepare for this scenario:

Review the Acceptance Letter: Carefully read through the acceptance letter to understand any specific instructions or requirements. Take note of important dates and deadlines.

Evaluating Your Options: If you are accepted to multiple programs, first review the pros and cons of attending each school. Consider the curriculum, faculty profile, location, program length, cost, and scholarship and research opportunities, as well as opportunities for hands-on experience.

Listening to Your Gut: Sometimes, the best decision comes from listening to your intuition. If one program feels like a better fit, there might be something to that instinct. Don't rush your decision. Give yourself the space to consider your options and come to a decision that feels right for you. Once you've gathered all the information, weighed your options, and considered your feelings, it's time to decide. It may feel daunting, but remember, this is a big step towards fulfilling your dream of becoming an NP. No matter what decision you make, take the time to celebrate this achievement.

Financial Planning:[1] Assess your financial situation. Determine tuition costs, fees, and any financial aid or scholarships you've secured. Create a budget and explore options for funding your education, including student loans or grants.

Housing and Relocation: If your program requires relocation, start researching housing options in the new location. Consider factors like proximity to the campus, cost, and amenities. Begin the process of securing housing well in advance.

Notify Current Employer: If you are working, let your employer know about your acceptance into the program. If it requires you to resign, discuss your departure date and any transitional responsibilities. More information is provided in the section, 'Partnering with Your Employer.'

Academic Preparation: Reach out to the program coordinator or advisor to inquire about any pre-program coursework or reading materials. Start preparing academically for the upcoming challenges.

Scenario 3: Navigating Rejection or No Response

While you hope for acceptance into your desired NP program, it's essential to be prepared for the possibility of receiving a rejection letter. Here's how to prepare for this scenario:

Anticipate Emotions: Understand that receiving a rejection letter can be emotionally challenging. Be prepared to face feelings of disappointment and self-doubt. Recognizing that these emotions are natural can help you cope better. Embracing them is a courageous step toward repositioning yourself for future applications. Before reapplying, take time to understand these feelings; they offer valuable insights into your motivations and aspirations, which will be powerful assets on your journey to becoming a nurse practitioner.

Seek Feedback: Reach out to the NP program admissions office to request feedback on your application. Constructive feedback can provide valuable insights into areas for improvement in future applications.

Reapplying: If becoming a nurse practitioner remains your aspiration, don't be discouraged from reapplying in the future. Use this time to strengthen your application, whether it's improving your academic record or gaining additional clinical experience.

Partnering with Your Employer

Partnering with your employer during the waiting period strategically aligns your current position with your educational goal. This alignment is important because it makes sure your education is supported by the people you work with every day. This is why I encourage you to maintain your current position if possible, as the rapport you have already established can lead to a flexible schedule or amendment in responsibilities.

I experienced this during my first semester in NP school. My supervisor agreed to change my schedule from five 8-hour shifts to four 10-hour shifts. This adjustment was quickly made after my initial request, as detailed in **Table 8**, and my supervisor was very supportive and excited about me becoming an NP.

The following semester I switched jobs to work closer to home which allowed me more time to study. That was very short lived, mainly due to my new supervisor's lack of support with me attending NP school. She went beyond expressing doubts and actively tried to convince me not to proceed with the NP program. Faced with this dire situation, I explained how far I had progressed in the program and offered to step down from my managerial role to lessen my responsibilities if adjusting my schedule was unfeasible. Despite this, she declined, and following our conversation, the work environment became noticeably uncomfortable. Eventually, I made the tough decision to leave and joined a well-known insurance company as a nurse case manager. What initially felt like a setback became a significant turning point in my life. This change came with the flexibility I needed to study efficiently and a $22,000 salary increase. Above all, it had a positive impact on my family and personal life, allowing me more quality time to spend with my husband and daughter as well as indulge in self-care for work-life harmony.

Your path may be different. It might involve tough choices like leaving a job, or stepping back from a high-responsibility role. These decisions, while difficult, are sometimes necessary to create the space and environment needed for your academic success. Remember, each step, each decision, brings its own lessons and opportunities, shaping you into the nurse practitioner you aspire to be.

Understanding the importance of these dynamics, it's essential to effectively communicate with your employer. To assist in this process, I have provided structured templates: 'Initial Email to Supervisor #1' to be sent upon program acceptance (**Table 9**), a direct 'Email to Supervisor #2' as a follow-up (**Table 10**), 'No Response: Follow-Up Email to Supervisor' to be sent about a week after the initial email (**Table 11**), 'Email to Supervisor's Boss if No Response Received' (**Table 12**). These templates are designed to help you articulate your intentions and needs clearly and professionally, ensuring they are well-understood.

Initiate a Dialogue with Your Employer: Schedule a meeting or initiate a conversation with your supervisor to discuss your application to an NP program and how it aligns with your professional goal (**Table 9**). Be clear about potential changes in your schedule, responsibilities, or availability that may arise if accepted.

Table 9. Initial Email to Supervisor #1

Initial Email to Supervisor #1 (to be sent upon program acceptance)
Subject: Schedule Change Request for Educational Advancement Dear [Supervisor's Name], I am reaching out to discuss a potential adjustment to my work schedule as I embark on my educational journey towards becoming a Nurse Practitioner (NP). The commitment to lifelong learning has always been integral to my professional development, and I believe this pursuit aligns with our organization's values. The course schedule requires me to attend classes on [specific days and times]. I have reviewed my current work schedule and believe that with some minor adjustments, I can continue to fulfill my responsibilities without any negative impact on our team. Would it be possible to schedule a meeting at your earliest convenience to discuss the details? Your support in this matter is deeply appreciated, and I look forward to collaborating on a solution that benefits both my professional growth and our shared goals. Thank you for your consideration. Best regards,   [Your Full Name]

Table 10. Direct Email to Supervisor #2

Initial Email to Supervisor #2 (straightforward)

Subject: Schedule Change Request for Educational Advancement

Dear [Supervisor's Name],

I'm pursuing further education to enhance my skills in [specific area], and I need to discuss a potential modification to my work schedule. This education aligns with our team's goals and will contribute to our success.

Could we schedule a brief meeting to discuss the necessary adjustments? Your support is vital, and I'm eager to work with you on this.

Thank you for your consideration.

Best regards,

[Your Full Name]

Table 11. No response Follow up email to Supervisor

No Response: Follow up Email to Supervisor (to be sent about one week after the initial email)
Subject: Follow-Up: Schedule Change Request for Educational Advancement Dear [Supervisor's Name], Thank you for your attention to this matter. I am writing to follow up on my previous email regarding a potential adjustment to my work schedule to accommodate my educational pursuits. Understanding that you have a demanding schedule, I want to emphasize my commitment to finding a solution that aligns with our team's needs. Your guidance on this matter is essential, and I would greatly appreciate the opportunity to discuss this further. If you require any additional information or have any concerns, please don't hesitate to reach out. I look forward to hearing from you soon. Best regards, [Your Full Name]

Table 12. Email to Supervisor's Boss if No Response Received

Email to Supervisor's Boss if No Response Received After Follow-Up (to be sent two weeks after the follow-up email to supervisor)
Subject: Assistance Required: Schedule Adjustment for Education Pursuit Dear [Supervisor's Boss Name], I hope this email finds you well. I am reaching out to seek your assistance with a matter I have been discussing with [Supervisor's Name]. I have sent a request and a follow-up email to discuss an adjustment to my work schedule to accommodate my educational pursuits towards becoming a Nurse Practitioner (NP), but I have not received a response. As I embark on this academic journey, I remain committed to my professional responsibilities and believe that with some minor adjustments, there will be no negative impact on our team's performance. I would be most grateful if you could provide guidance on how to proceed or assist in facilitating a dialogue with [Supervisor's Name]. I have attached copies of my previous correspondence for your reference. Thank you very much for your attention to this matter, and I look forward to hearing from you. Sincerely, [Your Full Name] [Your Title] [Contact Information] Attachments: [Attach previous emails]

Table 13. Follow-up Email

Initial Follow-Up Email (to be sent a week after submitting the application)
Subject: Application Follow-Up - [Your Full Name] Dear [Recipient's Name], I hope this email finds you well. I recently submitted my application for the Family Nurse Practitioner or Doctor of Nursing Practice in Transformational Leadership program on [Date Submitted]. I am writing to confirm that you received my application and that there are no outstanding items that need my attention. Thank you for your time and consideration. I eagerly await any updates regarding my application status. Best regards,   [Your Full Name]

Table 14. Additional Follow-up Email

Additional Follow-Up Email (to be sent 2-3 weeks after the initial follow-up if no response has been received)
Subject: Further Follow-Up - Application Status Inquiry - [Your Full Name] Dear [Recipient's Name], I hope this message finds you well. I'm writing to follow up on my previous email regarding my application for the Nurse Practitioner program at [University Name]. I am keen to know if there are any updates regarding my application status or if there is any additional information you require from me at this stage. I remain very interested in the opportunity to contribute to [University Name] and further my nursing education. I appreciate your time and consideration and look forward to hearing from you soon. Best regards, [Your Full Name]

Criminal Background Check

You will be asked to complete a background check which is a part of the enrollment process to screen for students who may be a risk to other students on campus. In NP school, it is more about the safety of the patients. The schools are particularly looking for convictions. Therefore, it is possible for a nurse to have been arrested in the past for a crime and not convicted. I suggest consulting with an attorney if you have a history that you are unsure would disqualify you as an applicant.

Understanding the Commitment

NP school is a serious commitment of time and resources. Be sure you are ready to commit and the rigors of the coursework, clinical hours, and likely some level of personal sacrifice. This is what this guide is about.

Getting Ready for NP School

You achieved a major milestone transforming from dreaming about becoming an NP to being accepted into NP school. This phase influences every aspect of your life in and out of school. It is not just about academic changes, it is a change in your personal and professional life. To prepare yourself for this new phase in your career, here are some steps to jumpstart NP school.

Prepare Your Family and Manage Competing Commitments: Involve your family and close friends in your journey. Talk about what NP school involves and the changes it will bring. Create a support network that understands and supports your goals.

Balance Work and School: Consider how NP school will fit with your current job and personal life. You might need to adjust your work hours or make changes in your personal routine for this new phase.

Prepare Your Finances: Carefully plan your finances for NP school. Budget for your education expenses and consider how a potential income change will affect your regular expenses like mortgages and loans. Another overlooked method is crowdfunding. Crowdfunding has become a popular method for raising money for your tuition as well as other pursuits.

Master Time Management: As you get ready for NP school, work on improving your time management. Organize your studies, work, and personal activities effectively to ensure success in the program.

Prioritize Self-Care: Remember, your physical and mental well-being are priority. Implement stress management practices and work towards maintaining a healthy lifestyle while in NP school.

Find Your Tribe: A strong support system is essential. Connect with fellow students and stay in touch with your family and friends for both emotional and practical support. For more strategies on building your tribe, revisit the networking section in Chapter 1.

Prepare for Clinical Hours: Plan for your clinical rotations, considering they might be at unconventional times or places. Think about travel arrangements, child care and pet care needs, and adjusting your work schedule to accommodate your new commitment.

Dr. Little's Prescription:

Complete the transition plan. Adhering to this timeline can lead to a more successful application process, aligning with the goals and ambitions of a prospective Nurse Practitioner.

Table 15. A Transition Plan Table for Progressing from Nurse Practitioner (NP) to an NP Applicant over a 9-12 Month Period

Task	Description	Timeline to complete
9-12 Months Before Application Deadline		
1. Identify Target Programs	Research and identify suitable NP programs.	2-4 weeks
2. Gather Transcripts and Credentials	Collect all relevant academic transcripts and professional certifications.	2-3 weeks
3. Register for Necessary Exams	Register for required entrance exams.	4-6 weeks
4. Explore Financial Aid Options	Explore and apply for scholarships, grants, and financial aid if needed.	Ongoing
6-9 Months Before Application Deadline		
5. Consult with Current Employer	Discuss intentions and needs with your supervisor.	1-2 weeks
6. Prepare Resume and CV	Update your resume and CV to reflect current skills and experiences.	1-2 weeks
7. Write Personal Statement	Draft and revise personal statements.	
8. Secure Letters of Recommendation	Request and collect recommendation letters.	
6-9 Months Before Application Deadline		
9. Apply for Financial Aid	Apply for necessary financial support.	
10. Build Network with Current NP Students	Connect with current students for insights.	
11. Prepare for Interviews	Practice and prepare for potential interviews.	

12. Submit Applications	Complete and submit applications to chosen programs.	
2-4 Months Before Application Deadline		
13. Notify Employer of Application Status	Keep the employer informed about application progress.	
14. Explore Housing and Relocation	Research housing if relocation is necessary.	
15. Develop a Budget Plan	Plan budget reflecting tuition and living expenses.	
16. Investigate Licensing Requirements	Understand specific licensing requirements.	
17. Plan for Work Transition	Create a work transition plan with your employer.	
After Application Submission		
18. Prepare for Acceptance Decision	Plan next steps for acceptance or waitlist scenarios.	
19. Evaluate Offers and Make Decision	Review acceptances and decide on a program.	

Glossary

Accreditation Commission for Education in Nursing (ACEN) - National accrediting agency for nursing programs under National League of Nursing (NLN)

Advanced Practice Registered Nurse (APRN) – a masters or doctorate prepared nurse who has received advanced didactic and clinical training. The four categories of APRNs include Nurse Practitioner (NP), Certified Nurse Midwife (CNM), Nurse Anesthetist (CRNA), and Clinical Nurse Specialist (CNS)

American Association of Nurse Practitioners (AANP)- National organization for Nurse Practitioners professionals.

American Nurse Credentialing Center (ANCC) – National certifying body for Registered and Advanced Practice nurses.

BSN to DNP - Advanced practice nursing track where a Bachelor of Science in Nursing degree bridges to a Doctor of Nursing Practice Degree

BSN to MSN – Advanced practice nursing track where a Bachelor of Science in Nursing degree bridges to a Master of Science Degree

Capstone Project – a senior exhibition or end of program design that illustrates students' abilities including critical thinking, problem-solving, public speaking, research skills, planning, goal setting.

Clinical Rotation - the hands-on training or theory application of NP students as a healthcare provider. Also called preceptorship, clinicals, or practicum for short.

Commission for Nursing Education (CNEA) - National accrediting agency for nursing programs

Commission on Collegiate Nursing Education (CCNE) - an autonomous accrediting agency, contributing to the improvement of the public's health. The Commission ensures the quality and integrity of baccalaureate, graduate, and residency programs in nursing.

Doctor of Nursing Practice (DNP) – A practice based terminal degree for nurses.

Examination Preparation (Exam Prep) – Also called "board preparation" which is a review of the national exam content that is required for Nurse Practitioner certification.

Full-Practice Authority – describes the state practice environment for nurse practitioners where no documentation of a collaborative agreement or supervising physician is required for them to practice independently.

Institutional Review Board (IRB) – a constituted group that reviews and monitors research involving human subjects. Each institution as its own IRB regulated by the U.S Food & Drug Administration (FDA)

Nurse Practitioner (NP) - An NP is a master's or doctorate-prepared advanced practice registered nurse authorized to diagnose, prescribe, and autonomously treat patients.

Nurse Practitioner Specialty - a population focus area of a Master of Science in Nursing degree program with a concentration in nurse practitioner; Family Nurse Practitioner (FNP), Women's health Nurse Practitioner (WHNP), Neonatal Nurse Practitioner (NNP), Pediatric Nurse Practitioner (PNP), Adult Gerontology Nurse Practitioner (AGNP), Psychiatric-Mental Health Nurse Practitioner (PMHNP), Acute Care Gerontology Nurse Practitioner (ACGNP)

Outcomes – the data or findings of a DNP or scholarly project that has been implemented.. Can be data found from surveys, observation, and test scores.

Preceptorship - the hands-on training or theory application of NP students as a healthcare provider. Is called "clinical rotation" or "practicum."

Prerequisite – in terms of education, a course or degree required as a prior condition for program admission.

Proprietary – an institution that operates as a business, and the product they sell is education; for-profit businesses which provide vocational education and training. Examples of Proprietary NP Schools include Chamberlain University, Walden University, Western Governors University

Reduced Practice – written agreement exists that specifies scope of practice and medical acts allowed with or without a general supervision requirement by a MD, DO, DDS, podiatrist or APRN; or direct supervision required in the presence of a licensed, MD, DO, DDS, podiatrist or APRN with or without a written practice agreement, or other conditions to practice.

Residency – post graduation program that provides an additional 12 to 24 months of clinical training in areas of community health, acute care, and specialized practices.

Restricted Practice – A written agreement exists that specifies scope of practice and medical acts allowed with or without a general supervision requirement by a MD, DO, DDS, podiatrist or APRN; or direct supervision required in the presence of a licensed, MD, DO, DDS, podiatrist or APRN with or without a written practice agreement, or other conditions to practice.

RN to MSN - Advanced practice nursing track where an Associate of Science in Nursing degree bridges to Doctor of Nursing Practice Degree.

Scholarly Project - senior exhibition or end of program design that illustrates students' abilities including critical thinking, problem-solving, public speaking, research skills, planning, goal setting. Is also called a "DNP Project" or Capstone."

Loan Forgiveness If you are employed by a government or not-for-profit organization, you may be able to receive loan forgiveness under the Public Service Loan Forgiveness (PSLF) Program.

PSLF forgives the remaining balance on your Direct Loans after you have made 120 qualifying monthly payments under a qualifying repayment plan while working full-time for a qualifying employer.

Tuition Reimbursement Many companies offer their employees some form of educational assistance. Tuition reimbursement plans allow workers to pursue specific degrees and certificates, with the company contributing a set amount of money.

Endnotes

1. El-Banna, MM, et al. "Does Prior RN Clinical Experience Predict Academic Success in Graduate Nurse Practitioner Programs?" Journal of Nursing Education, vol. 54, no. 5, May 2015, pp. 276-280, doi:10.3928/01484834-20150417-05.
2. Rich, Ellen R. "Does RN Experience Relate to NP Clinical Skills?" Nurse Practitioner, vol. 30, no. 12, Dec. 2005, pp. 53-56. PubMed, doi:10.1097/00006205-200512000-00009.
3. Lavoie, P., and Clark, S. P. "Educators' Perceptions of the Development of Clinical Judgment of Direct-Entry Students and Experienced RNs Enrolled in NP Programs." Journal of Nursing Regulation, vol. 12, no. 4, 2022, pp. 4-15, doi:10.1016/S2155-8256(22)00011-4.
4. Vanderbilt University. 'Pre-Specialty Nursing.' Vanderbilt University School of Nursing, 12, Jan. 2024, https://nursing.vanderbilt.edu/msn/prespecialty/index.php
5. "Best Healthcare Jobs." U.S. News & World Report, Jan. 2024, money.usnews.com/careers/best-jobs/rankings/best-healthcare-jobs
6. Lagasse, Jeff. "Nurse Practitioner Workforce Grows 8.5%." Healthcare Finance News, 14 Nov. 2023, www.healthcarefinancenews.com/news/nurse-practitioner-workforce-grows-85
7. U.S. Bureau of Labor Statistics. 'Nurse Practitioners.' Occupational Employment and Wage Statistics, May 2022, U.S. Bureau of Labor Statistics, www.bls.gov/oes/current/oes291171.htm
8. College Raptor Staff. "Types of Alternative Tuition Plans for College." College Raptor, 22 Dec. 2022,

     www.collegeraptor.com/paying-for-college/articles/financial-advice-planning/types-of-alternative-tuition-plans-for-college.
9. "Tuition-Free Nurse Practitioner Program at University of Pennsylvania." Clinical Advisor, www.clinicaladvisor.com/home/my-practice/nurse-practitioner-career-resources/tuition-free-np-program-penn-nursing-underserved-communities.
10. "Free Application for Federal Student Aid." Federal Student Aid, U.S. Department of Education, studentaid.gov/h/apply-for-aid/fafsa.
11. U.S. Army. 'Family Nurse Practitioner.' GoArmy.com, 2023, www.goarmy.com/careers-and-jobs/career-match/science-medicine/general-care/66p-family-nurse-practitioner.html
12. The University of Texas at Arlington. 'Military Opportunities for Nurse Practitioners.' UTA Online, 18 Dec. 2023, academicpartnerships.uta.edu/healthcare-nursing-online-programs/msn/fnp/military-opportunities-nurse-practitioner/
13. U.S. Air Force. 'Nursing Careers.' GoAirForce.com, 2023, www.airforce.com/careers/specialty-careers/healthcare/careers/nurse
14. United States Navy. 'Nursing Careers.' Navy.com, 2023 www.navy.com/careers-benefits/careers/medical/nursing.
15. USMilitary.com. 'Marine Corps Nursing Careers.' US Military, 28 May 2018, usmilitary.com/marine-corps-nurse
16. Myers & Briggs Foundation. "Myers & Briggs Foundation." The Myers & Briggs Foundation, 2023, www.myersbriggs.org
17. NERIS Analytics Limited. "16Personalities." 16Personalities, NERIS Analytics Limited, 2023, www.16personalities.com

Chapter 2

1. "Best Family Nurse Practitioner Programs." U.S. News & World Report, www.usnews.com/best-graduate-schools/top-nursing-schools/family-nursing-rankings.
2. Accreditation Commission for Education in Nursing. 'Accreditation Commission for Education in Nursing.' ACEN, 2023, www.acenursing.org.
3. "Commission on Collegiate Nursing Education Accredited Programs." American Association of Colleges of Nursing, www.aacnnursing.org/ccne-accreditation/find-accredited-programs.
4. National League for Nursing Commission for Nursing Education Accreditation (CNEA), cnea.nln.org.
5. CBS New York. "Lehman College Students Stunned To Learn School's Family Nurse Practitioner Program Accreditation Withdrawn." 4 Dec. 2020, www.cbsnews.com/newyork/news/lehman-college-family-nurse-practitioner-program-national-commission-on-collegiate-nursing-education.
6. "Shattered Dreams: Allow NYC Nurses to Become Board Certified." Change.org, 18 Dec. 2020, [www.change.org/p/commission-on-collegiate-nursing-education-shattered-dreams-allow-nyc-nurses-to-become-board-certified](https://www.change.org/p/commission-on-collegiate-nursing-education-shattered-dreams-allow-nyc-nurses-to-become-board-certified?utm_content=cl_sharecopy_26160742_en-US%3A5&recruiter=1167186748&utm_source=share_petition&utm_medium=copylink
7. Indeed Editorial Team. "Why Mission Statement is Important." Indeed, 3 Feb. 2023, www.indeed.com/career-advice/career-development/why-mission-statement-is-important
8. Georgia Baptist College of Nursing at Mercer University. 'Mission, Core Values, Vision and Goals.'

Mercer University, 2024, nursing.mercer.edu/about-the-college/mission-core-values-vision-and-goals.
9. "True claim: Some graduate schools are waiving GRE test requirements because of COVID-19." Reuters, 8 April 2020, www.reuters.com/article/uk-factcheck-coronavirus-gre-waive/true-claim-some-graduate-schools-are-waiving-gre-test-requirements-because-of-covid-19-idUSKCN21Q2Z6/.
10. AANPCB. 'How Examinations are Scored.' AANPCB, 18 Dec. 2023, www.aanpcert.org/certs/score
11. "American Nurses Credentialing Center (ANCC) Certifications ANA", https://www.nursingworld.org/our-certifications/. Accessed 18 Dec. 2023.
12. "Types of Nurse Practitioner Specialties." American Nurses Association, www.nursingworld.org/practice-policy/workforce/what-is-nursing/types-of-nurse-practitioner-specialties. Accessed 30 June 2023.
13. "What's a Nurse Practitioner?" AANP (American Association of Nurse Practitioners), https://www.aanp.org/about/all-about-nps/whats-a-nurse-practitioner. Accessed 30 June 2023.
14. Indeed Editorial Team. "Job Outlook: What it is and Why it's Important." Indeed, last updated 24 June 2022, www.indeed.com/career-advice/career-development/job-outlook-definition.
15. Indeed Editorial Team. "Best Careers for the Next 10 Years." Indeed, last updated 16 Mar. 2023, www.indeed.com/career-advice/career-development/best-careers-for-the-next-ten-years.
16. "Are You Considering a Career as an Adult-Gerontology Acute Care Nurse Practitioner?" American Association of Nurse Practitioners (AANP), https://www.aanp.org/news-feed/are-you-considering-a-career-as-an-acute-care-nurse-practitioner, Last Updated: 22 Jan. 2020, Retrieved: 9 Dec. 2023

17. "Evolution of the Gerontological Nurse Practitioner and the Gerontological Advanced Practice Nurses Association 1981—2020."Gerontological Advanced Practice Nurses Association, www.gapna.org/sites/default/files/documents/misc/GAPNAHistoricalBook.pdf
18. McComiskey, Carmel A. "The Role of the Nurse Practitioner: A 50-Year History: What Is Our Future?" Journal of Pediatric Surgical Nursing, vol. 7, no. 1, 2018, pp. 1-2, doi:10.1097/JPS.0000000000000158.
19. NONPF Statement - Reaffirming DNP Entry to Nurse Practitioner Practice by 2025." NONPF (National Organization of Nurse Practitioner Faculties), Sept. 2015, https://cdn.ymaws.com/www.nonpf.org/resource/resmgr/DNP/NONPFDNPStatementSept2015.pdf. Accessed 5 Dec. 2023
20. NONPF Statement - Reaffirming DNP Entry to Nurse Practitioner Practice by 2025." NONPF (National Organization of Nurse Practitioner Faculties), https://www.nonpf.org/news/638126/NONPF-Statement---Reaffirming-DNP-Entry-to-Nurse-Practitioner-Practice-by-2025-.htm. Accessed 5 Dec. 2023
21. "Commission on Graduates of Foreign Nursing Schools." www.cgfns.org.
22. Program with Carl Vinson VA Medical Center." The Den, 18 Dec. 2020, https://den.mercer.edu/college-of-nursing-to-offer-primary-care-nurse-practitioner-residency-program-with-carl-vinson-va-medical-center/. Accessed 15 Sept. 2023

Chapter 3

1. "Everything You Need to Know about College Transcripts." Southern Nazarene University, degrees.snu.edu/blog/everything-you-need-to-know-about-college-transcripts.

2. National Organization of Nurses with Disabilities. (n.d.). U.S. Department of Labor, Office of Disability Employment Policy. Retrieved from https://www.dol.gov/agencies/odep/alliances/previous/nond.
3. "History of Facebook: Facts and What's Happening." TheStreet, www.thestreet.com/technology/history-of-facebook-14740346.
4. "How to Take Professional Headshots with a Smart Phone." Headshots Inc., headshots-inc.com/blog/how-to-take-professional-headshots-at-home.

Chapter 5

1. Reese, Donna. "Best Ways to Get NP School Paid For." NursingProcess.org, [https://www.nursingprocess.org/best-ways-to-get-np-school-paid-for.html]. Accessed 1 April 2023

Glossary

1. Accreditation Commission for Education in Nursing. 'Accreditation Commission for Education in Nursing.' ACEN, 2024, www.acenursing.org.
2. American Association of Nurse Practitioners. 'State Practice Environment.' AANP, Oct. 2023, www.aanp.org/advocacy/state/state-practice-environment.

Resources

1. A & P Refresher. (n.d.). NurseHub. Retrieved from https://nursehub.com/courses/anatomy-physiology-refresher/.
2. "The Essentials Core Competencies for Professional Nursing Education." American Association of Colleges of Nursing, 6 Apr. 2021, www.aacnnursing.org/CCNE-Accreditation/Who-We-Are.
3. Perrla.(n.d.).Retrieved from https://www.perrla.com/#/.

About the Author

Dr. Patrice Little is a transformative figure in nurse practitioner (NP) education and practice, bringing a decade of family NP expertise to the forefront of professional advancement. As the founder of NP Student® she designed a framework that helps individuals become nurse practitioners (NPs), while overseeing and establishing pivotal educational and organizational partnerships.

Previously serving as a Senior Policy Advisor at the Campaign for Action, Dr. Little aided state APRN organizations in policy navigation regarding scope of practice, and worked to eliminate barriers in nursing education for pre-licensure students.

Her scholarly work includes contributions to "Advanced Practice Nursing Leadership: A Global Perspective" and "The Future of Nursing 2020-2030: Global Applications to Advance Health Equity," highlighting her dedication to nursing policy.

During the 2022 Legislative Session, Dr. Little served as a content producer with Georgia Public Broadcasting, demonstrating her communication skills and talent for making complex policy information understandable to the public. In addition, Dr. Little's participation in the Healing Politics Campaign

School emphasizes her dedication to political strategy and healthcare advocacy.

Dr. Little serves as United Advanced Practice Registered Nurses (UAPRN) Director at Large where she works to strengthen Georgia APRN's roles through advocacy, educational excellence, and media strategy.

She holds a DNP degree from Georgia Baptist College of Nursing of Mercer University, an MSN from Brenau University, and BS degrees in Biology/Pre-Medicine and Nursing from Georgia Southwestern State University. She is a member of the Atlanta Association of Black Journalists (AABJ), the American Association of Nurse Practitioners (AANP), and the Gwinnett/Forsyth Chapter of UAPRN.

Made in the USA
Columbia, SC
13 February 2024